Glimpses of
Our Past

Life Along
the Rivers

Jonita Mullins

Copyright 2015
Jonita Mullins
All Rights Reserved

ISBN 13: 978-0-9789740-3-9

ISBN 10: 0-9789740-3-4

First Printing, March 2015

Published by Jonita Mullins

From "Three Forks History"
Muskogee Phoenix
Reprinted with permission.

Printed in the U.S.A.

Glimpses of Our Past: Life Along the Rivers

Jonita Mullins

Table of Contents

1. Pre-History 7

2. European Control 15

3. Indian Country 25

4. The Golden Age 51

5. Indian Territory 77

6. The Twin Territories 109

7. Oklahoma's First Century 145

Index 177

Jonita Mullins

1

Pre-History

The Calf Creek People

The rivers of Oklahoma are what attracted the early people who inhabited the area, some residing here thousands of years ago. The earliest people were hunters who would find game at their favorite watering holes and would leave their spear points behind as evidence of the hunt.
An archeological discovery was made of an ancient bison skull found with a spear point thrust into it just below the horn. The skull was uncovered in the Arkansas River near Sand Springs in Tulsa County. The spear point belonged to the Calf Creek people, so named because the first spear point associated with these people was found in Calf Creek Cave in Searcy County, Arkansas.
It is believed that the Calf Creek were a nomadic tribe moving around the Arkansas River basin, following the migration of the bison. Their spear points were large and very unique. The stone workers would heat the rock before "knapping" it. Knapping is the process of flaking off the edges of a flat rock to create a razor-like sharpness. Heating the rock made it easier to break and the Calf Creek

people seem to have been the first to have developed this process.

Campsites of the Calf Creek people have been found in Muskogee and Haskell Counties. Yet, despite many such sites throughout Oklahoma associated with the Calf Creek people, very little is known about them. They were in this region for a relatively short period of time and then faded from view.

A more recent people to inhabit our area were the Mississippian Mound Builders who lived along the river banks in eastern Oklahoma. Their mounds are found along the Grand River in Mayes and Wagoner Counties and the Arkansas River in Muskogee and Sequoyah Counties.

Unlike previous cultures that relied primarily on hunting for food, the Mound Builders were farmers. They planted corn, squash, pumpkins, beans and sunflowers in the rich river bottom lands where they lived. They developed new methods of storing food and were involved in trade with other native peoples all across the North American continent.

The mounds were used as burial sites and also for ceremonies in their religion. Mounds might also have served as lookout points, helpful in tracking the movement of game or of enemy tribes. Some mounds served as lookout points long after their original builders were gone. In Wagoner County, a mound called Blue Mound was used as a lookout location by troops during the Civil War.

The Mound Builders in Oklahoma were of the Caddoan stock, and thus were likely ancestors of the Caddo and Wichita tribes of today. Mound Builders who settled east of the Mississippi River were ancestors of today's Muscogee (Creek) Nation.

The Mound culture had faded by the time Europeans were exploring the Three Rivers region. Members of the Caddo and Wichita tribes then were dominant in this area.

Mound Builders Left Visible Reminders of their Presence

Drive around certain parts of Oklahoma and you might see an odd shaped hill that seems out of place in the landscape. Chances are you may be seeing the remains of an ancient Indian mound created by people who lived in Oklahoma over a thousand years ago.

Known today as the Mississippian Mound Builders, these people settled along rivers that drained the Mississippi River Basin. In Oklahoma Mound Builders lived along the Grand River in Mayes and Wagoner Counties, the Arkansas River in Muskogee and Sequoyah Counties, the Poteau River in LeFlore County and the Little River in McCurtain County.

The best preserved site of the various mounds found in Oklahoma is near Spiro in LeFlore County. The Spiro Mounds have yielded a rich array of archeological treasure that reveals a sophisticated culture controlling the flow of trade throughout the Mississippi Basin. It has been referred to as the "King Tut" of the Arkansas River valley.

The twelve mounds in the Spiro complex also prove that these Mound Builders had a good knowledge of astronomy. Certain house mounds line up exactly with the rising or setting sun at the changing of the seasons. Perhaps the complex acted as a giant calendar, important for an agrarian people in knowing when best to plant their crops.

The Muscogee People's Legendary Beginnings

The origin of the Muscogee people is one of legend with many stories being passed down from generation to generation. The very word Muscogee or Muskoke as it was often spelled in earlier days has a certain mystery enshrouding it. No one seems to know exactly when the name was first used for the Creek people or what its literal meaning is.

On a map drawn by C.E. Creager, an early Congressman from Muskogee, a notation is made that suggests the word Muskoke comes from the Algonquin word maskeg, meaning "swamp." Since the Muscogee people settled in the rich delta lands of Florida, Georgia, Alabama and South Carolina, this may be a plausible explanation. The early Creeks were a confederation of many tribes or clans who lived along the rivers and built mounds for religious ceremony and burial.

But Creek poet Alexander Posey spoke of a different name and different legend of origin for his people. In 1902 a new town was founded west of Eufaula near the Canadian River on a new rail line being built westward out of Fort Smith. The town's name was Spokogee and according to Mr. Posey, this was the true name of his people predating the name Muscogee. He stated that the meaning of this word is "true blood." Another source suggests the name means prairie town.

The legend of the Muscogee people that Posey knew was that the Creek people had migrated from South America, forming a tribe from seven clans. These ancient people were a warlike group and they fought their way up the Atlantic coast through Mexico before eventually settling on the rivers of Alabama and Georgia.

When Indian Removal became U.S. policy in 1830, the Creeks, along with the other four southeastern tribes made the difficult trek to the Indian Territory. In their long-held tradition, the Creeks settled along the Arkansas and Canadian Rivers in their new homeland.

Oklahoma Saw the Migrations of Many People

While Oklahoma's history is filled with the dramatic and poignant story of the removal of the Five Civilized Tribes, that is not the beginning of Native American migrations to and through the state. Even before European settlement of the American continents, native tribes would often feel pressured to move to new localities.

Sometimes this pressure arose from natural conditions such as a flood or a prolonged drought. At other times, the pressure came from a rival tribe challenging them for the right to live or hunt in a certain area. Thus of the number of tribes that are considered native to Oklahoma such as the Caddo, Comanche, Wichita and Kiowa, all migrated to this area from somewhere else long before the Spanish and French were sending exploration parties into Oklahoma.

It is believed that the Caddoan people at one time lived along the Gulf Coast of Texas and Louisiana. By the time the Spanish were exploring this area, however, the Caddos had moved into the Red River valley. Perhaps the tropical storms and hurricanes that can plague the coastal region accounted for the Caddo migration. When French expeditions moved into the Oklahoma area, Caddoan tribes such as the Tawakoni and Wichita were living along the Canadian and Arkansas Rivers.

The Apaches are believed to have migrated northward from Mexico. They settled for a time in the western sections of Oklahoma, including the panhandle. But the Apaches were pushed out of the region by the Comanches who were a Shoshonean tribe moving into Oklahoma from the northwest and settling in the Wichita Mountain region.

Siouan tribes such as the Quapaw and Osage are thought to have lived in the southeastern United States centuries ago, but they were pushed westward by the

Muscogeean tribes such as the Creeks and Choctaws. They settled for a time in the Missouri area, but then split. The Quapaws moved south and settled along the Arkansas River and the Osage remained in Missouri on the Osage River before eventually moving into the Three Rivers region.

For a state that can proudly claim more Native American tribes than any other, we are actually a state of emigrants. Nearly all of our "native" tribes moved here from somewhere else. But what better place to finally settle in and call home than Oklahoma.

Moccasin Prints Were Carved at Highest Points around Muskogee

As Honor Heights Park in Muskogee was being developed an interesting discovery was made on Agency Hill. A large slab of sandstone rock somewhere on that promontory had several sets of what appeared to be moccasin prints carved into it. The prints were of several different sizes – depicting footprints belonging to men, women and children. Why these prints had been carved in the rock was a mystery.

Earlier, Creek Chief Pleasant Porter had been consulted about these mysterious prints. It was his opinion that the moccasin carvings were meant to be a type of directional sign. Perhaps the prints were intended to point the way for a party that would follow. In the opinion of General Porter, the fact that these prints were different sizes indicated that this was not a war party since it included women and children. It might have been directions for a hunting party passing through the Three Rivers region.

According to a 1930 *Muskogee Times-Democrat* article about the moccasin prints, they were not an isolated phenomenon. Another rock bearing carved prints had also existed at one time on Fern Mountain, another prominent landmark in the area. That rock was destroyed by people chipping away at it to collect a souvenir. The newspaper article stated that similar carvings had existed in other localities.

Historian Grant Foreman was called on to help study and protect the rock on Agency Hill with its curious carvings. Foreman made a rubbing of the prints and sent it to the Smithsonian Museum in Washington. Museum officials expressed an interest in the carvings, but could not offer an explanation as to their origins.

The Muskogee Historical Society, led by Grant Foreman, wanted to build some type of fence around the rock to protect it from people who were carving their initials into it. Whether the Society was successful in doing so is unknown.

At one time, Agency Hill was truly a landmark, rising above the treeless prairie that surrounded it. When the Union Agency was built on the hill in 1875, the building could be seen for some distance, just as the Jack C. Montgomery VA Medical Center can be seen there today.

From its height, cattle could be seen grazing in the distance when the area was open range land. It would not be surprising that a passing hunting party might camp on that hill. The height would give the hunters a view of game moving through the area and would also enable them to spot members of a rival tribe approaching their camp.

Perhaps the carvers of these moccasin prints simply wanted to leave a visible reminder that they had once stopped for a time at this beautiful place.

Jonita Mullins

2

European Control

Coronado's Search for Gold Brought Him to Oklahoma

Tantalizing rumors of great golden riches brought Francisco Vasquez de Coronado from his home in Mexico northward into the Rio Grande valley. His expedition had been paid for, in part, with his wife's money and he was determined not to return home without the great riches he sought. With a party of nearly 1500 soldiers, natives and slaves, he left Mexico.

Coronado first came to the "seven cities of Cibola" which turned out to be a group of Zuni pueblos in New Mexico. No gold was found here, but a foray by some of his men to the west did bring them to the Grand Canyon. Coronado's expeditionary force stopped at Cibola for the winter and quickly wore out their welcome with the native people. To encourage the Spanish force to move on, they told Coronado of the city of Quivira further to the north where great riches abounded. Coronado took the bait.

In April of 1541, the Spanish leader set out in a northeastward trek that took him into the Oklahoma panhandle. Here Coronado's men found a treeless stretch of land without a single distinguishing feature to serve as a guiding landmark. Men who left camp to hunt the roaming buffalo would find it difficult, even impossible, to find their way back. The travelers found it necessary to place stakes along their trail to act as landmarks. This gave the region the name "Llano Estacado," meaning Staked Plains.

Though the exact route Coronado traveled has long been debated, it is generally believed that his introduction to Oklahoma was only the 34-mile-wide panhandle of the state. Crossing through this "no man's land," the Spanish force arrived at Quivira in June of 1541.

This Wichita village of grass covered lodges was an important trade center on the plains, but it was no city of gold. This same tribal people also occupied the Three Rivers region of Oklahoma. As a Plains people, the Wichita roamed the southern prairie, hunting the buffalo.

Coronado claimed for Spain the land drained by the river on which the Wichita village sat. The river was the Arkansas and Coronado's claim brought Oklahoma and the Three Rivers under the flag of a European country for the first time.

Coronado returned to Mexico, again crossing through the Oklahoma panhandle. With no gold found, the Spanish showed little interest in further exploration of Oklahoma. They couldn't know of the gold of vast wheat fields or the black gold of enormous oil deposits that later explorers and settlers would discover in our great state.

French Made Trade Treaty in 1719

In early European exploration of the North American continent both the Spanish and French made forays into what is now Oklahoma, both claiming the territory as their own. In 1719, a French commandant named Bernard de la Harpe ventured northward from his trading post on the Red River. He had been granted a trading license by the French governor at New Orleans which then served as the French capital of La Louisiane.

La Harpe intended to find new trading partners to increase the volume of furs and hides being exported to Europe. These items, along with pecans, honey, salt and tobacco, were traded by the Indians for guns, ammunition, metalware, knives, axes, cloth and beads.

The French were determined to counterbalance the trade the Spanish had established with the western Plains tribes such as the Comanches and Kiowas. The Spanish occupied southern Texas, then considered a part of Mexico, in a string of small missions centered primarily in the Rio Grande valley. Except for a few exploratory excursions, the Spanish had virtually ignored the lands north of the Red River. It was in this region that La Harpe hoped to find new trading partners.

He and a small corps traveled north from the Red River, crossed the Canadian and then moved toward the Arkansas. They reached a Tawakoni village on the Arkansas River in early September. Along this route, they met with members of the Wichita Confederation – a band of several small tribes that shared a similar language and lived in permanent villages scattered on the banks of these rivers.

These Indian tribes – unlike the Plains tribes – were not nomadic. They did not live in teepees or travel the Great Plains following the migration of the buffalo. La Harpe described their homes as "dome-shaped houses of straw and reeds covered with earth."

La Harpe ended his push into northeastern Oklahoma near present day Haskell in Muskogee County. The Tawakoni spoke the Caddoan language and were hunters and farmers. They raised corn, beans, pumpkins and tobacco. They hunted bear and deer and enjoyed good fishing from the river.

La Harpe noted in his log of the journey that the Tawakoni were "a people of good sense." They were also noted for their friendliness as they welcomed visitors by washing their hands and feet, feeding them generously and offering them the best accommodations in the village.

La Harpe's party spent a few days with the Tawakoni, feasting on their best foods. While there, he instructed one of his men to "carve on a post the arms of the king and the company and the day and year of taking possession." And so the explorer claimed the area for France.

La Harpe never established a permanent trading post in Oklahoma, but his venture did open the area to trade with France. The Arkansas River became the highway that carried the natural riches of the region to the world.

French Responsible for Many Place Names in Oklahoma

While both Spain and England made claims on what became Oklahoma, neither European country made a great effort to explore the land here. The French were far more interested in the interior country north of the Red River than their rivals the Spanish and English. New Spain (now Mexico) claimed and defended only the territory south of that river and the French did not contest that claim.

Instead they sent numerous exploring and trading parties up the rivers that fed the Mississippi. This territory they named La Louisiane after the French king. Oklahoma was at the southern edge of the Louisiana territory and never attracted French settlements as did regions closer to the Mississippi.

In fact, there are few if any structures or permanent

evidence of the French presence in Oklahoma. What the French did leave in Oklahoma, however, were many place names that are either French or adaptations of French words.

In 1673, French explorer and priest, Father Jacques Marquette reached the mouth of a major river emptying into the Mississippi. He gave the river the name Arkansea after the Native Americans who lived along its banks. We know these Indians as the Quapaw, but the Osage called them the Arkakoze. Eventually the French adapted the river's name to Arkansas.

The Arkansas River basin was the next frontier to be explored by the French. This led them through mountain ranges they named the Ozarks and the Ouachitas. More rivers further into the interior of La Louisiane were given French names. The Poteau and Blanc (now called White) rivers were explored too. The falls on the Arkansas River near present day Webbers Falls were called La Cascade on early maps.

And why is it that Oklahoma has an Illinois River and Canadian River when we are nowhere near Illinois or Canada? The likely answer is that French explorers from Illinois and Canada named these rivers after their homeland. Another French-named river is the Verdigris, derived from two French words -- verde meaning green and gris meaning gray.

But there are only a few towns with French names in Oklahoma. This is because the French did not truly settle in the region. Manard is believed to be named for a French missionary named Pierre Menard. Chouteau and Salina are town names attributed to the French-American fur trader, A.P. Chouteau. And Sallisaw and Vian are towns with names derived from French words. Sallisaw is said to come from the word salaison, meaning salted meat and Vian from viande which means meat. Sounds like the French were hungry while visiting Sequoyah County.

Louisiana Purchase Helped Shape Our State

In April 1803, President Thomas Jefferson began negotiations with Napoleon Bonaparte of France to purchase 800,000 square miles of land extending from the Mississippi River to the Rocky Mountains. The cost was $15 million, roughly 4 cents per acre.

Jefferson had set out to purchase only New Orleans in order to keep trade and traffic on the Mississippi free and open. When Napoleon offered the whole of Louisiana Territory, Jefferson's envoy, James Monroe, jumped at the opportunity. The English version of the treaty was signed on May 2, 1803. With the stroke of a pen, the size of the United States was doubled.

The Louisiana Purchase has been called the greatest real estate deal in history. Fifteen states, including Oklahoma, were part of the Louisiana Purchase. It was a largely unexplored and unmapped territory. The southern boundary was the Red River, separating Oklahoma from Texas then held by the Spanish. The western boundary for what became Oklahoma was the 100th meridian, also a boundary with Texas.

All of Oklahoma was included in this land deal except for the strip of land today known as the Oklahoma panhandle. This land was a part of the Texas territory still under Spanish control. It would remain a part of Texas until 1845 when the Republic of Texas sought to join the Union as the state of Texas.

Under the Missouri Compromise, which sought to maintain a balance between slave states and free states, no state with boundaries north of the 36th parallel could enter the Union as a slave state. The Texas panhandle extended to the 37th parallel which was the southern boundary line of Kansas and Colorado Territories.

To be allowed to enter the Union as a slave state, Texas elected to lop off a 34-mile stretch of land between the 36th and 37th Parallels. This land which ran for 166 miles from the Cherokee Outlet to the New Mexico boundary was unattached to any territory for years and came to be called "no man's land." This area was attached to Oklahoma Territory in 1890.

President Jefferson sent several exploration parties into the Louisiana territory, the best know of which were the Lewis & Clark expedition and the Zebulon Pike expedition. A part of Pike's exploring party traveled through the Three Rivers area in 1806, making them the first Americans to record a visit to this area.

As a part of the historic Louisiana Purchase of 1803, the Three Rivers area, within this much larger piece of real estate, was among the first to be developed by Americans. The Three Rivers region epitomizes the American West with its Indians and fur traders, cowboys and cattle drives, the fort and the U.S. Cavalry, early pioneers and the railroad. In more ways than one, the Louisiana Purchase helped shape the state of Oklahoma.

Wichitas and Osages Dominated River Region

While the dramatic saga of the removal of the Five Tribes is perhaps the best known of Native American history in this region, it was not the earliest Indian history. The Three Rivers area was long inhabited by native people going back to at least 700 AD. At that time, the Mississippian Mound Builders were living here, creating the burial and religious mounds that were central to their advanced civilization.

Following the gradual demise of the Mound Builders society, came the Wichita Confederation. This was a loose alliance of tribes and clans who lived in permanent round thatch houses along the river bottomlands. They were farmers who raised squash, beans and corn and also hunters who relied heavily on the buffalo for food and clothing.

The Wichita were gradually pushed southward by the more aggressive Osage tribe. The first records about the Osage show them living in a large permanent village on the Osage River in what is now Missouri. The Osage depended upon the buffalo, but were also farmers. As the French and Americans began to establish trading posts along the Mississippi River, the Osage became astute traders as well.

In fact, the Osage became professional hunters, depending more and more upon their trade with Europeans and Americans for their existence. But game grew scarce in their traditional hunting grounds so they began to move further west and south in hunting expeditions.

This led the Osage into the Three Rivers area. Because of an abundance of water and salt, the area also had an abundance of game. By the mid-1700s, the Osage were spending much of their time in the Three Rivers region, camping between the Verdigris and Six Bulls (now called Grand) Rivers. Their trade trail back to Missouri was so often used that it became the first "highway" in this region and was known as the Osage Trace.

In the late 1700s, the Osage were led by three chiefs – Pawhuska, Claremont (for whom the town of Claremore was named) and Cashesegra. Pawhuska was the principal chief, but Cashesegra led a young and aggressive band of the Osage that came to be called "the Arkansas Band." Sometime between 1780 and 1802, Cashesegra led his group to settle permanently in the Three Rivers area. Their village was located across the river from where Fort Gibson would later be built. A.P. Chouteau purchased a trading post at Three Forks and it served also as the Osage Agency, with Chouteau acting as the U.S. government agent to the tribe.

In 1816, the Osage sold their land along the Three Rivers to the United States in a deal negotiated by William Lovely and called Lovely's Purchase. Later this land would be given to the western Cherokees. The Osage were settled on a reservation in Kansas and their dominance in the Three Rivers region came to an end.

Early River Travel Was Hampered by Rough Waters

It's hard to imagine today, but waterfalls on the Arkansas and Verdigris Rivers once made navigation difficult and sometimes even impossible. Travelers in canoes or pirogues (hollowed out logs) could portage around the waterfalls, but when the heavier and much larger flatboats, keelboats and steamboats began to ply the rivers, the tumbling water was a major obstacle. Thus in the early days, the waterfalls became the "end of the way" for folks traveling by river.

But what was an obstacle for travelers was an opportunity for traders and small communities developed at the waterfalls and became the destination point for keelboats and steamboats. On the Verdigris River, the falls occurred just after the river took a big turn southward before joining the Arkansas River at the Three Forks. Here Falls City started and this little town took on several locations and names throughout the years, but all were in sight of the "Falls of the Verdigris." Today this town is called Okay. The Falls are no longer visible.

On the Arkansas River, the waterfall was a more spectacular display of nature's wild, untamed beauty. Called "La Cascade" on early maps of the area, this waterfall had a drop of around seven feet. When river levels were high in the fall and spring, the drop was not nearly as dramatic and navigation over the falls was possible. In the dry summer months, travel would come to a halt at La Cascade.

It is uncertain who first noted the waterfall, but since it was given the name La Cascade, it was probably a French explorer. The first American to document the waterfall was Lt. James Wilkinson who was part of the Zebulon Pike Expedition sent out by President Thomas Jefferson to locate the source of the Arkansas River. Wilkinson and a group of five enlisted men passed La Cascade in December of 1806.

An English naturalist named Thomas Nuttall explored the region in 1819 and kept meticulous records of what he encountered out on the frontier. He also noted the waterfall on the Arkansas, stating that the boat ran aground at the waterfall, but because the water level was particularly high, he and his party were able to continue upriver.

A trading community developed at the Arkansas Falls just as it had near the Falls of the Verdigris. Here a Cherokee leader named Walter Webber settled in 1829. He operated a trading post that did a very good business at this location. Gradually the waterfall began to be called Webber's Falls because everyone traveling up the river would stop at Webber's trading post. Eventually the community that grew up around Webber's trading post was given the name Webbers Falls.

The waterfalls on the Arkansas and Verdigris Rivers no longer pose a problem for inland water travel. The McClellan-Kerr Navigation System overcame the waterfalls with a lock at Webbers Falls and by dredging a new channel for the Verdigris River to bypass the falls.

3

Indian Country

Remnants of old Salt Works Remain Today

The abundance of salt springs found in the Three Rivers region was one of the natural resource that drew both people and animals to northeastern Oklahoma. Native Americans mined the salt from these springs and used it not only for preserving food but also as a trade commodity with other tribes, as well as with the French, Spanish and English.

Animals were also drawn to the salt springs because they need salt in their diet and their instinct would lead them to the springs. This abundance of game in the Three Rivers area was what made the fur trade so lucrative here. Even the Osage Trace, Oklahoma's first road, developed because the Osage would travel into the Three Rivers area for the salt found here as well as for the good hunting.

Salt mining could be considered one of Oklahoma's first industries, developed long before Oklahoma or even Indian Territory was established. A salt mining business existed at a spring near Mazie before 1820. It was called the Neosho operation and was run by two partners, but little else is known about it. By the time the Union Mission was established near the Mazie spring in 1821, the Neosho operation was already out of business.

Two brothers named Richard and Mark Bean purchased the salt kettles from the Mazie spring and set up a salt works of their own on a spring near the Illinois River in 1820. Their tidy little farm, being one of only a few in this area at that time, was frequently visited by explorers to the region. The Beans built a spring house and furnace near the salt spring. Using large iron kettles, they would boil the water from the spring until it had evaporated and the salt was left. The Beans could get a bushel of salt from 55 gallons of saltwater. They would sell the salt for $1 per bushel and the military post at Fort Smith was their primary customer.

The Beans were forced to give up their salt works in 1828 when the land they had settled on was given to the Cherokees by the federal government. Nearly everyone already settled in the area were required to leave and as compensation they were given land in Arkansas Territory. The Cherokee Nation then gave the Bean salt works to the tribal member Walter Webber.

Another large salt works on the Illinois River was operated by a man named Mackey. His operation was about seven or eight miles further upstream from the Beans (about 10 miles from present day Gore). Like the Beans' operation, Mackey's farm was also a major stopping point on the road between Fort Smith and Fort Gibson.

The Mackey salt works continued operation until 1864 when it was destroyed by federal troops to prevent its capture by Confederates. After the war, the kettles were patched and used by local Cherokees. One of the huge iron kettles from Mackey's salt works can still be viewed on the campus of Bacone College. Another salt works kettle is displayed at the Five Civilized Tribes Museum.

The Frontier Merged Many Cultures

The story of the American frontier is one of many cultures, creeds and colors all coming together -- interacting with one another and sometimes clashing with one another. The early efforts at exploring and mapping the new boundaries of America were typical of the true western story. European, Latin, African and Native Americans were all a part of this history.

There are many references to black and Latino explorers and fur traders found in the journals and other early writings of the American West. Since early fur trade in this state was centered in the Three Rivers region, we can assume that from the time explorers and fur traders first pushed into this area, people of all colors were a part this era.

In 1719, French commander Bernard de la Harpe entered the Three Rivers area with an exploration party of about 10 men. La Harpe notes in his journal of the expedition that two of his party were black and were always well received in the Indian villages they visited.

Major Jacob Fowler led an expedition through the Three Rivers area in 1821, employing a local fur trader named Hugh Glenn to act as his guide. Fowler's records of the journey indicate that he had a personal slave named Paul (Fowler spelled his named Pall) who accompanied him. Paul had his own gun, money and horse and his opinion was sought and respected by other members of the exploring party. In the rugged western wilderness, where everyone's survival depended upon the cooperation and respect of the entire group, color and class distinctions seemed less important than intelligence and skill.

Trade trails crossed Oklahoma between the United States and Mexican-held territories in the southwest. Many Mexican "mule skinners" carried freight between trade centers such as St. Louis and Santa Fe, crossing through

Oklahoma. Many gold and silver Mexican coins have been found in trade areas such as Three Forks and rumors of Mexican gold mines existing in the territory have long circulated.

Fur trading posts lined the banks of the Three Rivers for many years and they were a gathering place for all manner of people. The keelboats that plied the rivers carrying furs bound for New Orleans were often manned by Creoles (of African, Spanish or French descent), who poled the long heavy boats to the rhythm of traditional African songs.

When Washington Irving visited Fort Gibson in 1832, he also stopped at the trading post of A.P. Chouteau on the banks of the Verdigris River near present-day Okay. Irving described the scene there in his book *A Tour on the Prairies*. He contrasted the Osages, clad in blankets and leggings, with the newly arrived Creeks who dressed in colorful calico shirts and turbans.

Irving also mentioned a large number of Creoles and "negroes of every hue," particularly noting the hard-working African blacksmith who happened to be shoeing a horse at the time. Since Chouteau operated a boat-building yard on the river, many of these men were possibly employed at building and operating the boats for his fur trade.

On the frontier of early America, there was opportunity for people of many ethnic backgrounds. While clashes between the cultures certainly occurred, the fight for survival meant cooperation and mutual respect were just as often a part of this great American story.

First American Exploration of Oklahoma Brought Attention to the Rivers

After the Louisiana Purchase in 1803, explorers were sent out by President Thomas Jefferson to map the region because the boundaries had never been clearly established. While Lewis and Clark were dispatched to explore the northern rivers of the territory, Zebulon Pike was commissioned to travel and map the southern rivers.

In the summer of 1806, Pike left St. Louis and traveled across the prairie to the Arkansas River (in what is now Kansas). They arrived at the Big Bend of the Arkansas in late fall. While Pike continued up the river, he dispatched his second in command, James Wilkinson, to travel down the Arkansas.

Wilkinson and a party of five soldiers followed the Arkansas River south, traveling in pirogues, hollowed out from cottonwood trees. Wilkinson's journal of this exploration is the first American account of Northeastern Oklahoma. He reported passing several Osage villages as well as a number of Cherokee and Choctaw hunting parties.

Travel down the Arkansas was slow going as the weather began to turn colder. On occasion, the explorers would have to chop through layers of ice formed on the river. Rain and snow hampered them as well. At one point, a pirogue turned over in the icy water and dumped much of their supplies. Had it not been for a friendly band of Osages re-supplying the Americans, they might not have survived the journey.

On December 23, 1906, Wilkinson's party rested at an Osage village located between the Verdigris and Grand Rivers where they join the Arkansas. Wilkinson found the Osages eager to trade with the Americans and they asked that a trading post be established in the area. Wilkinson would make such a recommendation in his report to the President, but that report actually came a little late.

As Wilkinson's group continued down the Arkansas, they met Joseph Bogey traveling upriver from Arkansas Post, a settlement at the mouth of the Arkansas River. Bogey, a Frenchman who had been trading along the Arkansas for a number of years, had secured a license to trade with the Osages in the Three Rivers area.

With a large boat loaded with goods for trade, and a crew of 12 men, Bogey was braving the late December cold to travel to the mouth of the Verdigris. He entered this river and found a deep stretch of still waters below the Verdigris Falls. Here he built his trading post at a spot where his flatboats could land.

Bogey's post was the first at Three Forks and one of the first in the entire state of Oklahoma. Within the next ten years, another dozen traders would move into the Three Rivers area, making it one of the most important fur trading centers west of the Mississippi.

Arkansas River Connects Oklahoma to the World

Long before ox-drawn wagons or railroad steam engines brought travelers to the Wild West, the rivers were the most important means of transportation. The early settlement of this area, where the Arkansas, Grand and Verdigris Rivers join together, was due, in large part, to those navigable rivers. The rivers made this region an ideal site for commerce that was unsurpassed in the entire southwest.

Because of the ancient mounds found along the rivers, we know that early Native Americans inhabited this area over 1,000 years ago. The bottom land was fertile and the rivers made trade possible to a surprisingly large region.

Later, descendants of these mound builders and early European explorers traveled the rivers by canoe or pirogue. The pirogue had no seating and required the traveler kneel and paddle. Such travel was uncomfortable, but usually quicker than traveling over land.

By the time Fort Gibson was established on the Grand River in 1824, the keelboat had become the preferred mode of river travel. This type of boat was a small craft about seventy feet in length. Without engine, these boats were brought upstream by physical labor. This usually meant horse or mule teams along the riverbanks would pull the boats by a rawhide towline. Sometimes crews of twenty to thirty men would haul the boats upstream.

As early as 1828, steamboats were navigating the Arkansas River. The first steamboat to land in the Three Rivers area was the *Facility*, bringing 780 Creeks to the Creek Agency on the Verdigris River. By the 1840s, steamboat navigation was in its heyday. There were 22 steamboat landings on the Arkansas River between Fort Smith and Fort Gibson. Steamboat companies in New Orleans regularly advertised Creek Agency as one of their destination points.

Most of these steamboats were small and they were often wrecked on submerged trees during times of low water. The falls at Webbers Falls also proved to be an obstacle during low water periods. Steamboats sometimes had to be towed by mule teams to get them past the rough current at the falls. If water levels fell too low, travel would simple halt until rains brought the river levels up again.

For many years, the Three Forks location was considered the end of the line for river travel by steamboat or other large craft. But in the 1870s, merchants in Kansas utilized the Arkansas River by sending flatboats and steamboats downstream with loads of produce and other goods. The steamboat *Aunt Sally* managed to travel upstream all the way to Arkansas City, Kansas in 1878.

Gradually steamboat travel declined, especially after the railroad built through the Three Rivers area. In the early 1900s, progressive citizens in Muskogee began to push for a return of river navigation. They commissioned the *City of Muskogee*, a steamboat that traveled the Arkansas during Oklahoma's early oil boom days.

The push for improved river navigation continued, and in 1968 the McClellan-Kerr Navigation System was completed and Muskogee and Catoosa became port cities. The Arkansas and Verdigris Rivers today link the Three Rivers area with the Mississippi River and the world.

Pryor Creek Named for National Hero

When the Lewis & Clark Expedition began in 1804, the entire country waited with expectation to learn what these two explorers would discover as they crossed the American continent. The Corps of Discovery, as their expedition came to be called, was made up of military men who had experience in frontier exploration. The frontier at that time was anything west of the Appalachians. One of the sergeants recruited for the Lewis and Clark expedition was Nathaniel Pryor.

We know little of Nathaniel Pryor's early life except that he was a descendant of the great chief Powhatan and born in Virginia. He may have married around age 23. However, only single men were recruited for the Corps of Discovery so it is believed that Pryor had been widowed by the time Captain William Clark asked him to join the expedition. Pryor was recruited at Louisville, Kentucky in October 1803 and was made a sergeant in charge of the keelboat that carried their supplies up the Missouri River.

Pryor traveled across the continent of North America with Lewis and Clark, enduring sickness, hunger, cold and all the other deprivations of the difficult journey.

Many times the two captains commended Pryor in their journals. When the Corps of Discovery returned to St. Louis, every member of the expedition was hailed as a hero and parties were thrown in their honor wherever they traveled.

Pryor continued in military service in the First U.S. Infantry. He served under General Andrew Jackson at the Battle of New Orleans in the War of 1812. He rose to the rank of captain in the Forty-Fourth Infantry and for the remainder of his life was addressed as Captain Pryor.

In 1816, Pryor entered business with a fur trader named Samuel Richards at the French-American settlement of Arkansas Post located near the mouth of the Arkansas River. He remained there for a few years, and then obtained a license to trade with the Osage at a post on the Verdigris River at the Three Forks.

Here Captain Pryor married an Osage woman and enjoyed good trade relations with Chief Claremont and his band of Osage. Pryor quickly established himself as a highly respected leader among the American traders who were beginning to populate the Three Rivers area. His experience with Lewis and Clark had been valuable training for surviving the wilderness and dealing with the native people.

In 1819, Pryor served as a guide for Thomas Nuttall, a Harvard scientist who was researching the flora and fauna of the Indian country. He also helped with the establishment of the Union Mission in 1820 among the Osage.

In 1827, his former captain, William Clark appointed Pryor as acting U.S. sub-agent to the Osage. So well-respected was Pryor, that both Sam Houston and Captain Matthew Arbuckle at Fort Gibson petitioned to make this a permanent position and it was in 1831. Unfortunately Pryor died shortly afterwards at his home on

Pryor Creek. The creek and the town of Pryor Creek take their names from this American hero.

Three Rivers Brought Earliest Settlers

The Three Rivers area was little more than a remote wilderness when it became a part of the United States in 1803. Osage and Wichita tribes considered the area their winter hunting grounds, but true permanent settlement was sparse.

Within a decade of the U.S. purchase of Louisiana Territory, however, the area around the juncture of the three rivers was filling up fast. Like a magnet, the three rivers seemed to pull traders into the region, all hoping to profit from the abundance of fur-bearing animals that inhabited the spring-watered prairie.

One of the traders who came early to this region was Samuel Morton Rutherford, who had been born in Virginia around 1795. At age 12, he and his family settled in Tennessee and he completed his schooling there. When he reached 17, he joined the Tennessee Volunteers and fought in the Battle of New Orleans in the War of 1812.

That battle against the British to protect the important shipping route along the Mississippi River brought many young soldiers into the Louisiana and Arkansas territories. Here Rutherford met Nathaniel Pryor who also fought at New Orleans under General Andrew Jackson.

These two young men, probably with many other militiamen mustered out after the war, decided to settle at Arkansas Post and try their hand at the fur trade. Arkansas Post sat near the mouth of the Arkansas River where it joined the Mississippi.

Between 1816 and 1819, Pryor and Rutherford along with other traders such as Samuel Richards and

Robert Mosby French worked the fur trade between Arkansas Post and Three Forks. By 1819 Rutherford and French were settled on the west bank of the Verdigris River.

Another fur trader and soldier, A.P. Chouteau, also had trading posts at Three Forks as well as others near rivers in the region. The Chouteau family was one of the wealthiest fur trading enterprises in the American West.

Rutherford moved back to Arkansas for a time and quickly moved into positions of authority there. His experience in trading among the Indians brought him back to Indian Territory when he was appointed as a special agent to the Choctaws. He lived at Sculleyville while in this position and also when serving as Superintendent of Indian Affairs.

In his later years, Rutherford settled at Fort Smith, Arkansas and was buried at the Oak Cemetery located there. His descendants, however, continued to reside in Indian Territory as did the descendants of A.P. Chouteau. The Morton and Chouteau families were among the oldest in Indian Territory because they made the Three Rivers region their home well before the Indian Removals brought the Five Civilized Tribes to Indian Territory.

Soldiers Spent Christmas Building Southwest's First Fort

It was Christmas Day, but there was no turkey or ham with all the trimmings for the crack Rifle Regiment commanded by Major William Bradford. The 64-man unit had spent the past two months poling and pulling a loaded keelboat down the Mississippi River and then up the Arkansas River. They had arrived at a bluff overlooking the Arkansas known as Belle Point this December in 1817.

Here they would immediately begin work on building a fort.

The need for a military presence in the "Indian Country" had increased over the past years since the U.S. government had signed a series of treaties with the Cherokees encouraging them to settle west of the Mississippi. In 1812, a migration of around 2,000 Cherokees had begun. These Native Americans left lands in the Blue Ridge Mountains for lands in the Ozarks. It might have been an ideal move had it not been for the fact that they were settling on lands long hunted by the Osages.

The Osages lived in the Three Rivers region, having a large village between the Verdigris and Grand Rivers just north of where the Port of Muskogee is now located. The Osages resisted the Cherokee incursion into their hunting grounds. Hunting parties often turned into war parties as the two tribes clashed.

As early as 1814, Cherokee agent William Lovely had recommended to the government that a fort be built somewhere along the Osage-Cherokee boundary. Such a military presence, he hoped, would curb fighting between the two tribes and would also discourage non-Indian settlement on lands granted to the Indians.

It wasn't until 1817, that the request for a fort was met. Secretary of War Richard Graham ordered General Andrew Jackson to build such an army post. Jackson, in turn passed the orders to General Thomas Smith who dispatched Major Bradford and his Rifle Regiment into the region.

Bradford's men arrived at the mouth of the Arkansas in November, some sickened and in need of rest. Bradford sent Major Stephen Long, a topographical engineer, and a small contingent of soldiers to scout the best location for the fort. Long chose Belle Point because of its commanding view of the Arkansas River. Bradford and his remaining men arrived here on Christmas to begin construction of Fort Smith.

It was only a few years later that Fort Smith's second commander, Colonel Matthew Arbuckle, deemed the fort too far removed from the center of Indian settlement. In 1824, he brought his Seventh Infantry to Three Forks to build Cantonment Gibson.

Mission Work Was Difficult on the Frontier

The Three Rivers area was the first location of a mission in the "Indian Country." Still considered a part of Arkansas Territory in 1820, the Three Forks region was then home to the Osage tribe. Here the Union Mission was established about 25 miles north of the junction of the rivers on the west bank of the Grand River (then called the Neosho) near where Mazie is located today.

Just getting to the grounds that the Osages had granted for use as a mission proved to be quite an ordeal for those first missionaries. They traveled by river on the Ohio, Mississippi, Arkansas and Grand using keelboats that either had to be rowed or pulled by mules along the shore. Because the keelboat was a heavy craft, travel could not be made in the summer when water levels were low. So they arrived at the Union Mission site in November 1820 in chilly and rainy weather.

The first arrivals, including the mission superintendent Epaphras Chapman, set about to build housing for the remainder of the "mission family" who were to follow. Though the mission grounds of about a thousand acres were described as a "good country" for raising crops and livestock, it was open prairie with little timber. The wood needed for buildings had to be cut and hauled across the Grand River.

In February 1821, the rest of the mission party arrived but they had already lost two of their members who died on the arduous trip in the cold, wet conditions. This is one of the first instances of non-Indian women and children settling in the "wilderness" of what would become Oklahoma.

Sickness was a constant problem among the mission group most of whom were from New England and completely unprepared for the harsh living conditions on the frontier. Despite having a medical doctor at the mission, several members of the party died in the intervening years of a disease called the "intermittent" (a malarial-type fever).

The purpose of Union Mission was primarily one of education. These members of the Congregational Church hoped to teach the Osage not only the basics of reading and writing but also skills such as farming, carpentry, and home management. As such, only a couple of members of the mission family were ministers. The rest were teachers, a farmer, carpenter, blacksmith, stonemason, the doctor and several women to care for the students and oversee the household.

Unfortunately for these hardy missionaries, the Osages who visited the mission came more out of curiosity than from a commitment to their own education. Most were not yet interested in adopting the "white ways" of homesteading and farming. For its 15 years of existence, Union Mission never saw many students come to learn to read or how to use a plow or to operate a gristmill.

Yet Union Mission was significant for more reasons than just being first. The missionaries earned the respect of the surrounding Osage villages as they literally "broke ground" on the open prairie. The mission put nearly a hundred acres of land into production, growing corn, potatoes and cotton and demonstrating to the native people the ways of farming. The mission also opened its school to the Cherokees, traditional enemies of the Osage, and as the children of these two tribes sat in classes together, tolerance and understanding were taught as well as the alphabet.

The work of the Union Mission never proved easy, but the courageous men and women who did that work have earned a place of respect in Three Rivers history.

River Region Was a Place of Abundance

From the tales written by early soldiers, explorers and settlers, we know that the Three Rivers region could be described with one word – abundance. It is hard to imagine, in our modern life with long ribbons of highway and endless miles of power lines and huge dams taming the rivers, that the area was treeless prairie meeting woodland hills.

The trees of the forests towered above the rivers and streams, the prairie rolled across the landscape as far as the eye could see, and the cane growing along the rivers was so thick that the only way through it was to hack away at it with machetes. Nature left to its own devises was prolific, wild and beautiful, inspiring awe among the first explorers here.

The abundance of wildlife also included a vast variety of animals in the Three Rivers area. Well-watered and fertile, this region could support huge numbers of deer, elk and buffalo. A good number of salt springs in the area also attracted wildlife and early hunters could easily follow their trails to their favorite watering hole.

Grant Foreman wrote in his history of Fort Gibson that the first soldiers who came to build the fort found themselves sharing the neighborhood with black bears and packs of wolves. The sleek panthers' screams in the wilderness would set their hair on end and have them reaching for a nearby rifle.

The surrounding prairie was grazing land for large herds of wild horses, deer, and even buffalo though that huge beast normally migrated further west of this region. Also abundant in the area before it began to be more heavily settled was the wild hog, a kin to the razorbacks of the Ozarks. Called "slow deer" by hunters, hogs rooted around in the woods, feasting on walnuts, hickory nuts, berries and pecans.

Fowl of every variety were also abundant in this area. When Washington Irving made his tour on the prairies in October 1832, he wrote about seeing huge flocks of migrating geese that would fill the sky with their noisy honking. Irving also reported seeing wood ducks on the many ponds he passed as he traveled through almost uncharted areas of Oklahoma.

Turkeys, prairie chickens, wild pigeons and parakeets were also thick upon the prairie and no one with any hunting prowess at all would ever want for food. Grant Foreman observed a shipment of 4,000 pigeons being loaded on a railcar for transport back east. It was not uncommon for hunters to catch 300 to 400 of these birds in a single day.

Another abundance of nature observed by Irving were the swarms of honeybees that made their hives in hollowed, decaying trees in the woods. The Army Rangers whom Irving traveled with would cut down twenty trees at a time to gather the golden honey stored by the bees. He stated that his party could cross streams on huge beaver dams, so sturdily built that they would support both the riders and their horses.

Bees weren't all that swarmed in the area. Mosquitoes were a pesky problem of massive proportions, not just because of their annoying bite, but also because they spread disease, especially among the soldiers at Fort Gibson. And when the first railroad was being built across Indian Territory in 1872, it was the mosquito that became one of the biggest obstacles the tracklayers had to deal with.

For the early inhabitants along the rivers, the abundance found here made it an attractive place to settle. That's why the history of this area stretches back for hundreds of years and is some of the most fascinating in the state of Oklahoma.

Chouteau Family Led Fur Trade Along the Rivers

When Colonel Matthew Arbuckle ascended the Arkansas River in 1824, looking for a site to locate a fort in the Three Rivers area, he originally intended to build on the Verdigris River. But he found that the best boat landing on that river was already occupied by a bustling community of fur traders, so the fort was placed on the Grand River instead.

Along the Verdigris, above its confluence with the Arkansas, a number of trading posts were engaged in a thriving business. The earliest had been established in late 1806 by Joseph Bogey and he was followed by other traders such as Nathaniel Pryor, Hugh Glenn and Samuel Rutherford. According to historian Grant Foreman this fur trading community was the earliest non-Indian settlement located in what became Oklahoma.

The largest and most prosperous of the fur trading establishments in the area was without dispute that of A.P. Chouteau. Colonel Chouteau was a descendant of the wealthy French family who had helped to establish St. Louis. He had graduated from West Point in 1806, but had retired from the military to join his family in trade with the Indians, primarily the Osage.

In fact, the Chouteaus had turned their trade with the Osages in Missouri into one of the largest fur trading outfits in America, rivaling that of John Jacob Astor. And along the way, they had established themselves as experts in Indian affairs. It was to the Chouteaus that Lewis and Clark had turned for assistance in outfitting their Corps of Discovery in 1804.

A.P. Chouteau took responsibility for the family's fur trade in the Three Rivers area. By the time Fort Gibson was established in 1824, he had taken a small trading post on the Verdigris and had built it to one of the largest on the western frontier. He employed a large number of men, of all races, to work in his fur factory and his shipyard.

Chouteau would build the boats on which he shipped his peltries to either New Orleans or St. Louis. He hired skilled river men to navigate the tricky Mississippi and upon reaching their destination, they would sell the furs and the wood used to build the boat. Then they would load a keelboat with supplies, such as casks of nails and of liquor, and would return to Three Forks.

Besides being regarded as an astute businessman, Colonel Chouteau was also a recognized authority in Indian Territory. Until his death in 1838, Chouteau was frequently involved in treaty negotiations among various Indian tribes. The military at Fort Gibson welcomed his visits and would often consult with him on matters relating to Native Americans. Officials in Washington respected his judgment and often deferred decisions on Indian affairs to him. It is not an exaggeration to say that the Chouteaus were one of the most important families on the American frontier.

Western Arkansas Territory Encompassed the Indian Country

When Arkansas Territory was established in 1819, its western boundary extended well into what today is

Oklahoma. The Three Rivers area was located in what was called Lovely County, Arkansas Territory, named for Cherokee agent William Lovely.

This piece of real estate was a much disputed land area. The Osages, Cherokees, Choctaws and a few American settlers all felt a claim on Lovely County. It led to frequent armed conflict, particularly between the Osages and Cherokees.

This conflict was one of the main reasons why Fort Gibson was established in Lovely County. It was hoped that the presence of the U.S. Seventh Infantry here would discourage the raids being carried out between the two Native American tribes.

John Nicks was First Sutler and First Postmaster

Coming to Fort Gibson with the Seventh Infantry was a sutler named John Nicks. He was born during the American Revolution in 1781 in North Carolina. Little is known of his early life except that he received a better than average education. He entered the Army in 1808 at the age of 27 and saw distinguished service during the War of 1812.

Like so many young soldiers who were mustered out of the Army after that war, he continued to live on the frontier, but Nicks chose to re-apply for service. He was assigned to the Seventh Infantry and rose to the rank of Lieutenant Colonel by 1819 before he was honorably discharged in 1821.

Nicks accepted the appointment as sutler for the Seventh Infantry. A sutler was a merchant who had a contract with a military post to provide soldiers with food, non-military clothing, liquor, toiletries and other sundries.

He also opened a mercantile in the town of Fort Smith with a partner named John Rogers. Nicks was a shrewd businessman, but well-liked by his patrons. Nicks also joined the Arkansas militia and achieved the rank of Brigadier General. In 1823, he was elected to the Arkansas Territorial Legislature.

When the Seventh Infantry moved further west to establish Fort Gibson, Nicks made the move as well with his store and his bride Sarah. He continued to operate his Fort Smith mercantile. Ironically he found another trade partner in the new town of Fort Gibson who was also named John Rogers and they established a mercantile there. The two partners to Nicks were not related to one another. Both stores were called Nicks and Rogers.

Because Arkansas Territory at that time extended 40 miles west of Fort Gibson, John Nicks continued to served in the Arkansas Legislature. He was appointed to a commission to find a suitable location for a county seat for Lovely County which included a good portion of what is northeastern Oklahoma today. The site chosen was on Sallisaw Creek in what is now Sequoyah County and was named Nicksville and its post office was established in 1828.

Nicksville served as county seat for only a brief time. In 1828, a treaty between the Osages and Cherokees gave Lovely County to the Cherokees. The Osages were moved to a reservation in Kansas and all non-Indian settlers were required to leave Lovely County. The Arkansas Territorial boundary was also moved to the present line between Arkansas and Oklahoma.

When a road was completed between Fort Smith and Fort Gibson in 1827, the mail route was extended to Gibson and John Nicks was appointed the first postmaster at the Fort. Because he was better educated than many of the frontiersmen and enlisted men around the post, Nicks was involved with much of the treaty making that took place at Fort Gibson in its early years. Many of these treaties bear Nicks' signature as a witness.

John Nicks met Sarah Perkins in Fort Smith and married her in 1824. They had two children named Eliza and John Quinton. At Nicks' death from pneumonia in 1831, his wife Sarah was allowed to continue to run the sutler store until a new sutler could be appointed. Some say this made Sarah the first woman sutler for the Army, but others argue that she was never officially named sutler.

Nicks was buried in the old fort cemetery and his grave was re-interred in the Fort Gibson National Cemetery after the Civil War. Over the years, his headstone fell into disrepair and was almost lost. Historian Grant Foreman petitioned the military to set a new headstone in place and this was done in 1932. This stone can be viewed in the Officer's Circle at the National Cemetery today.

The town of Nicksville was not completely abandoned. The Cherokees moved Dwight Mission from near Russellville, Arkansas to the old Nicksville buildings in 1830. The mission managed to continue in operation even during Civil War. While those old Nicksville buildings are all gone now, the mission grounds are still used today by the Presbyterian Church.

Riverboat Traffic Was a Challenging Business

When you consider how difficult travel upon the rivers was in the early days of the frontier, you have to wonder why anyone would attempt it. But the simple fact was that all modes of transportation were difficult in a land with few roads and no bridges. Traffic upon the "water highway," though challenging, was often the least cumbersome route to take.

The invention of the steam engine and its application to river travel opened up new possibilities for trade in the Three Rivers region. Up until that time – the late 1820s – river travel was made primarily by keel boats.

The power that moved these boats upstream was manpower, by rowing, poling or pulling the boats. Travel had to be done in the winter when river levels were high – but not at flood stage as they often were in the spring and fall.

For years the head of navigation on the Arkansas River was downstream from Three Forks. Keelboats usually stopped at Fort Smith and supplies were then brought by wagon to Fort Gibson. Steam transportation pushed the head of navigation further upstream because the steam engine could provide greater power for passing the rough water at Webbers Falls.

One of the first steamboats to begin regular trade between New Orleans and Fort Gibson was the *Facility*. Its captain was Philip Pennywit, a native of Virginia who had spent most of his life working as a riverman. He had entered the trade as a young man and worked on the Ohio and Mississippi Rivers between Cincinnati and New Orleans for a number of years.

Finally he had his own steamboat – the *Facility* – and it became a well-known boat on the Arkansas River. Pennywit was, in fact, a pioneer in steam travel on the Arkansas. Most river captains were content to deliver their cargo to Fort Smith and not risk further travel upstream. But Captain Pennywit was determined to push the boundaries westward.

In 1828, he agreed to pull two keelboats behind the *Facility* all the way to Fort Gibson. The passengers on these keelboats were Creeks immigrating from Georgia and Alabama to their new lands in Indian Territory. No steamboat had reached Fort Gibson before this time. Captain Pennywit arrived in Little Rock with no trouble but had to wait a month at this port for the water to rise. He then continued upstream but ran aground in the vicinity of today's Kerr Lake and had to wait for the water to rise again.

Finally he arrived at Fort Gibson in February of 1828. The *Facility* was the first steamboat to reach this destination and Three Forks then became the head of navigation on the Arkansas. Captain Pennywit attempted several other trips to Fort Gibson that year, but with limited success. On occasion he would have to drop anchor at Sallisaw Creek or Dardenelle and transfer his cargo to land.

Pennywit went on to operate other boats on the Arkansas, including the *Waverly* and the *Neosho*, before he retired from the river trade in 1847 and settled in Van Buren, Arkansas.

Dwight Mission Important to Early Cherokee Education

Dwight Mission was the second mission to be established in Oklahoma among the Cherokees. The mission had originally been located in Arkansas on the Illinois Bayou near Russellville. It was named for Timothy Dwight, a president of Yale College, and founder of the American Board of Missions.

A band of the Cherokees had settled in Arkansas around 1812, many living along the Arkansas River where it flowed between the Ozark and Ouachita Mountains. Their chief was Tahlonteeskee. He returned east in 1817 to the main body of the Cherokees and requested that a mission school be established among the Western Cherokees.

Rev. Cephas Washburn and Rev. Alfred Finney were dispatched from Brainerd Mission, a Presbyterian station in Georgia to begin the work in Arkansas. They arrived in early January 1820 and spent several months scouting the area for a location for the school.

The Dwight Mission school opened in January 1822 with fifteen Cherokee students. Within a few years nearly a hundred students were attending the school. Like the missions in Georgia, this school used the syllabary created by Sequoyah.

It is believed that Sequoyah's home, where he developed the written Cherokee language, was located at Illinois Bayou near where Dwight Mission was established. Other Cherokee leaders associated with the Mission included Takatoka and John Jolly, the adopted father of Sam Houston.

A settlement developed around Dwight Mission and it gained a post office in 1823. This community served as a port on the Arkansas River and a stage stop for early travelers. Non-Indian settlers in the area also sent their children to school at Dwight Mission.

In an 1828 treaty, the Western Cherokees agreed to move out of Arkansas to Indian Territory. Dwight Mission moved with the Cherokees and a suitable site for the school was located in what is today Sequoyah County. The director, Cephas Washburn, purchased buildings for the mission at the community of Nicksville. Today the closest community to the mission site is Marble City.

Washburn worked at Dwight Mission until 1840. The mission itself managed to continue in operation even during Civil War, but eventually it was closed. Today the old Nicksville buildings have long since disappeared, but the mission grounds continue in use for Presbyterian conferences and retreats.

Oklahoma's Oldest Fort Created Its Oldest Town

Like many other towns on the western frontier, Fort Gibson began as a camp surrounding the actual fort that was built on the Grand River in 1824. All military posts had camp followers who wanted to do business with the government, its soldiers and their families. These included legitimate businesses such as mercantiles, blacksmiths, laundries, and hostelries and perhaps a few illegitimate ones including gambling tents and saloons.

By 1827, Fort Gibson had the first post office in what would become Indian Territory and then Oklahoma. It was called Cantonment Gibson, Cherokee Nation at first, and John Nicks served as the first postmaster. Since this was a politically appointed position, postmasters changed often as did the location of the post office. It has been said that nearly every older building in downtown Fort Gibson housed the post office at one time or another.

In 1857, the United States abandoned Fort Gibson as a military post and its ownership reverted to the Cherokee Nation. At that time, the Cherokee Council created the town of Kee-too-wah, platted town lots on the military grounds and offered the barracks and other buildings for sale to Cherokees. Records are sketchy, but it is generally believed that such notable Cherokees as William Ross, Dennis Bushyhead and Daniel Ross purchased the military buildings.

The town of Kee-too-wah never actually developed, however. In 1862, federal troops under Colonel W.A. Phillips once again occupied Fort Gibson to control Indian Territory during the Civil War. The fort was closed again in 1871, but troops were occasionally stationed there for the next 20 years whenever the need for a military presence might arise. The famed Buffalo Soldiers of the Ninth and Tenth Cavalry were among those occupying Fort Gibson at various times.

Like most towns in the American West, Fort Gibson was greatly impacted by the coming of the railroad. When the Kansas & Arkansas Valley Railroad passed near Fort Gibson, the businesses of the town eventually all moved closer to the tracks. The two locations of the town were then referred to as "Old Town" and "New Town." Later many black-owned businesses located in the "Old Town." The old and new town sites were incorporated as the city of Fort Gibson in 1898 when the Curtis Act allowed for town incorporation.

In 1904 all the land that had belonged to the fort was included in the town site survey conducted by the Department of the Interior. Most of it had passed from the Cherokee Nation to private ownership by this time. However, the "Old Stockade" area was reserved for a park and purchased by the town. It was first called Sam Houston Park in a nod to the fact that the famous Texan had once lived just across the river from the fort.

In 1897, Lura Rowland a young blind woman from Arkansas began a school for blind students in the old barracks. This school later moved to Muskogee and became the Oklahoma School for the Blind.

Fort Gibson had its struggles with disastrous fires, floods, and the Great Depression. During World War II, the town's population swelled with the coming of Camp Gruber to nearby Braggs. Today Fort Gibson is a town steeped in history and distinguished as Oklahoma's oldest town.

4

The Golden Age

Indian Agents Were Men of Influence and Power

As soon as the Louisiana Purchase was completed in 1803, the federal government began to establish its presence in the Three Rivers area through Indian agents. This is one of the reasons that Three Forks was so significant to the development of Indian Territory. The Indian agent, as the government's representative to the native people, became one of the most important and influential men in the Territory.

Agents were appointed by the President and often the position was a reward for military service or a political perk. It was the agent's responsibility to negotiate treaties and settle disputes. With the authority of the federal government behind him, he would often be the keeper of the peace when tensions arose between the tribes or between Indians and non-Indians.

These agents often worked to further educational opportunities and expand trade among the Indians they served. Of course, some Indian agents looked out for their own interests rather than that of the Indians, but on the whole these agents did strive to improve conditions in Indian Territory.

Many agents were well-known individuals who had already established a name for themselves before coming to Indian Territory. Others remained in Indian Territory after serving as agent to continue in positions of influence and importance.

One of the earliest agents for the Osages was A.P. Chouteau for whom the town of Chouteau is named. His trading post at Three Forks was usually referred to as the Osage Agency. This same trading post later served as the first Creek Agency.

Another Osage agent was Nathaniel Pryor for whom the town of Pryor Creek is named. Pryor was a soldier who had been part of the Lewis and Clark expedition in 1804. He also served at the Battle of New Orleans under General Andrew Jackson. After he left the military, Pryor also established a trading post at the Three Forks among the Osages.

Another trader/agent in the Three Forks region was Sam Houston who acted as an agent for the Cherokees. Houston only lived in Indian Territory three years, but during that time made a trip to Washington, D.C. on behalf of the Cherokees. He also attended most of the treaty meetings held at Fort Gibson during his brief stay here.

The government consolidated the agencies of the Five Tribes in 1875 and a Union Agency was established in Muskogee. The agents appointed to the Union Agency included Colonel Robert L. Owen who later became one of the first Senators from Oklahoma.

Leo Bennett was an editor of the *Muskogee Phoenix* and the *Eufaula Indian Journal* before serving as the Union agent. He later served as federal marshal in Indian Territory. A third agent, Col. Dew M. Wisdom later served as Muskogee's second mayor.

Sam Houston Settled Between the Rivers

Called "The Raven" by his Cherokee friends, Sam Houston had left a rising political career in Tennessee after resigning abruptly from the office of Governor in that state. He moved west to escape the scandal of a failed marriage to live among the Cherokees he had grown up with back in Tennessee.

After settling in the Cherokee Nation, Houston married a Cherokee woman, Diana Rogers, and established a trading post and home that he named Wigwam Neosho. The site of his trading post was near present-day Okay and from his home he could watch the riverboat traffic on both the Verdigris and Neosho (now Grand) Rivers where they flow into the Arkansas. He surely also would have noticed the growing stream of settlers traveling southward along the Texas Road which forded the Arkansas River near his home.

On his arrival in Indian Territory, Houston almost immediately plunged into tribal affairs, often advising the commander at Fort Gibson on dealings with the Indians. His Cherokee friends asked him to travel with their second chief Blackcoat to Washington to address issues of Indian sovereignty.

After working with the Cherokee three years, Houston left Indian Territory and Diana for a new life in Texas. He later sent for Diana to join him, but she refused, not feeling she would fit in the white world and not wanting to leave her own people.

Houston quickly involved himself in the volatile politics of Texas. Being officially a part of Mexico, the Texas territory was rapidly being settled by Americans who clamored for independence. Houston, who had served in the military during the War of 1812, was appointed general in a growing Texas army.

He served as a delegate to the Convention that

declared Texas independence in 1836. Houston was promptly named commander of all the Texas forces. Just over a month later, Houston and his men defeated Mexican General Santa Anna at the Battle of San Jacinto which decisively won Texas independence from Mexico.

In the fall of that same year, Sam Houston was elected first president of the Republic of Texas. He served two terms as president and the town of Houston was established as the Republic's capital. After Texas joined the Union in 1845, Houston represented the state as a Senator.

He fell from political favor, however, because he opposed Texas' secession from the Union to join the Confederacy. Houston was removed from office in 1861 and died just two years later in July 1863. His son Temple Houston was a prominent lawyer in Oklahoma Territory in later years.

McIntosh an Important Name in Creek History

The name McIntosh is one of significance in the history of the Creek Nation. Though sometimes controversial figures, the McIntoshes have been leaders among the Creeks for several generations.

The patriarch of the McIntosh family was William McIntosh, the son of a Scottish trader and full-blood Creek woman named Senoia. He was born in 1775 in Wetumpka, Georgia. Growing up in a mixed-race family, he was comfortable with both cultures and could speak both Muscogee and English. When he was 25, William was selected as a Micco (town chief) of the town of Coweta, Georgia. He quickly became a recognized leader among the Lower Creeks and frequently negotiated with the Georgia government on behalf of his people. He was a prosperous trader, owning two plantations and operating a ferry at Indian Springs.

In 1825, at the age of 50, William was persuaded (some sources say he was bribed) to sign the Treaty of Indian Springs, ceding all Creek land in Georgia in exchange for land in Indian Territory. This treaty was later declared void and was immediately opposed by the Upper Creeks and even many Lower Creeks. A Creek Council declared McIntosh's actions treason and sentenced him to death. A group of his opponents went to his home late one night, set fire to his house and then shot him as he fled the flames.

Ironically, the Creeks later signed a treaty that had less favorable terms than the Indian Springs Treaty. In it they ceded away all their land in Georgia and Alabama. The Creeks from Coweta and other Lower Towns began their removal to Indian Territory in 1828. William's son, Chilly McIntosh, made several trips bringing Creek emigrants to their new land.

William's younger brother Roley McIntosh stepped into a leadership role among the Lower Creeks who were also called the McIntosh Creeks. Roley was the first Creek to serve as chief in Indian Territory and he held this position for thirty-one years. The McIntosh family, along with many Lower Creek families settled on the Verdigris and Arkansas Rivers in closely connected plantations.

At the outbreak of the Civil War, two of William McIntosh's sons, Daniel and Chilly, formed battle regiments in the Confederate Army. The First and Second Creek Cavalry Regiments took part in several battles including Pea Ridge and Honey Springs. Late in the war, Daniel McIntosh was organizing a third regiment, which would have given him the rank of Brigadier General, but the war ended before he was awarded that rank.

Following the Civil War, the McIntosh family settled in the Checotah and Eufaula area and at statehood the county containing these two towns was given the name McIntosh.

Other descendants of William McIntosh continued to be leaders in tribal affairs. Albert "Cheesie" McIntosh, his grandson, was an attorney who practiced law in Indian Territory. Albert represented the Creek Nation at the Sequoyah Convention in Muskogee in 1905 and the Oklahoma Constitutional Convention in Guthrie. A great-grandson of William's, Waldo McIntosh, served as principal chief of the Creek Nation from 1961 to 1971. And a great-great-grandson, Chinnubbie McIntosh was a Creek district judge and served on the Creek Council.

Tribes Built Along the Rivers

The Muscogee (Creek) Tribe is descended from an ancient people known as mound builders. These early Native Americans settled in the river valleys of the Mississippi basin. When Europeans began to establish their American colonies, they gave the Muscogee Tribe the name Creek because these native people built their towns along the banks of rivers and tributary creeks.

In fact, to further define the tribe they were referred to as Upper Creeks – those living along rivers from northwestern Georgia to central Alabama – and the Lower Creeks who lived further southeast.

The Creeks built their tribal government around their towns. Each town had its own chief or king. The members of the town remained members even if they moved or intermarried with someone from another tribe.

When the Creeks were removed to Indian Territory, they continued the tribal tradition of settling their towns along a river. The Upper Creeks established new towns along the Canadian River and the Lower Creeks settled near the Arkansas and Verdigris Rivers.

Many of these towns have the same names as those used in Alabama and Georgia, although often with different spellings.

Once settled in Indian Territory, the Creeks began to hold a National Council at High Springs, a central location within the Creek Nation. Each town would send a representative to this council that met on a hill in what today is Muskogee County.

This location became known as "the council hill" and the town of Council Hill takes its name from that site.

The National Council had been established in part to try to mend a rift among the Creeks that the removal to Indian Territory had created. The Lower Creeks had been mostly in favor of the removal, wanting to distance themselves from the encroaching European settlers. The Upper Creeks had opposed removal and resisted it for several years before being forced to make the long journey to new lands west of the Mississippi.

For a time, harmony was restored, but the Civil War ended this period of peace and prosperity for the Muscogee people. After the war, the tribe again worked for reconciliation among its members and set up a new government.

The people adopted a constitution that established the office of principal chief and second chief as well as a legislative and judicial branch of the government. The tribal legislature consisted of a House of Kings and House of Warriors. Representatives were sent to the legislature from the tribal towns.

To vote in elections, every Creek man had to return to his tribal town. The candidates for office would line up in the center of town. The men would cast their vote by lining up behind the candidate of their choice, and the town's king would count heads to determine the winner.

Government business of the Creek Nation was conducted at the Creek Council House, which is still in

Okmulgee, the Creek national capital. The tribal government was dissolved by the U.S. Congress in 1901 with a new treaty negotiated by the Dawes Commission. The Creeks adopted a new constitution in the 1970s.

Nathan Boone Surveyed Creek-Cherokee Boundary

In 1826, the Creeks signed a treaty agreeing to give up their lands in Georgia and Alabama for lands of their choice in Indian Territory. They sent out an exploring party who determined that the best location was in the rich bottomlands of the Arkansas and Verdigris Rivers. By 1828 nearly 2,000 Creeks had arrived in Indian Territory and settled on these chosen lands, putting them into cultivation.

That same year, the U.S. made a treaty with the Cherokees living then in Arkansas Territory which gave them lands the Creeks had already claimed. As the Cherokees began to move into Indian Territory there was an immediate dispute over land claims. Both tribes could point to treaties giving the same land to each of them. The Creeks were especially anxious to see the matter settled because they had already invested much effort in improving the land and building their homes on it.

The government appointed a commission to travel to Indian Territory and negotiate a settlement of this land dispute. This Indian Affairs Commission consisted of Henry Ellsworth, Montford Stokes and John Schermerhorn. The three-man commission arrived at Fork Gibson in late 1832 and immediately began to work for a resolution of the conflict.

In February 1833, the U.S. signed new treaties with the Creeks and the Cherokees setting forth a rough boundary line between the two tribes which ran from the

Canadian River at the mouth of the North Fork to the Arkansas River at the mouth of the Grand River.

To develop a more exact boundary line, the government hired a young soldier who had arrived at Fort Gibson in command of a company of Rangers. Captain Nathan Boone, son of the famous woodsman and explorer Daniel Boone, had extensive surveying experience. He was also regarded as every bit the expert woodsman as his father was and he knew the geography of the southwest as well as any other soldier stationed at the fort.

During March and April of 1833, Boone established the boundary between the Creek and Cherokee tribes which still applies today. Beginning on March 28, at the mouth of the North Fork of the Canadian, he planted a cedar post to mark the beginning corner. Then he set stones as mile markers along the 38 miles north to a spot on the south bank of the Arkansas River opposite of the mouth of the Grand River. This would be where the Port of Muskogee is located today. Boone set a second post here, to mark the north corner of the boundary.

Boone kept a field journal of his survey and noted the type of soil and kinds of trees located at each mile marker. A part of the Boone boundary line serves today as the eastern boundary of Civitan Park in Muskogee across from the Oklahoma School for the Blind.

Creeks Unite after Travel to Oklahoma

The Native American tribe known as the Muscogee or Creek Nation traces its ancestry back to more than 500 years ago. Known as the Mound Builders, these ancient ancestors of the Creeks are believed to have migrated from Mexico into what became the southeastern United States. They settled along river banks and constructed elaborate earthen pyramids called Mounds. Over time, these mound areas developed into towns and the Creeks occupied river bottoms in Alabama, Georgia, Florida and South Carolina.

The Creeks originally were a confederation of several small tribes or clans who all shared a similar culture and language – the Muscogee language. Each of these tribes or clans established their own tribal town and the towns each had their own political autonomy with their own chief (called a micco). The English colonists tended to lump all of these clans together and called them the Creeks, because they built their towns along rivers and creeks.

Most of the Creek population was concentrated into two geographical areas. The English called the inhabitants of the towns in northern Georgia and Alabama on the Tallapoosa and Coosa rivers, Upper Creeks. Those who lived to the southeast, on the Chattahoochee and Flint rivers were called the Lower Creeks.

Due to their closeness to the colonists, the Lower Creeks experienced more intermarriage and greater assimilation to American culture, including building large plantations and using slave labor. The Upper towns were less changed by Euro-American influences and maintained the old traditions, politics and social structures.

By 1825, the Creeks had ceded small parcels of land to the state of Georgia in a series of treaties. The leader of the Lower Creeks was William McIntosh who was of Scottish and Creek descent. He believed, and many Lower Creeks agreed with him, that the best thing for the tribe to do was to give up all their lands in Georgia for lands west of the Mississippi.

McIntosh signed the Treaty of Indian Springs agreeing to those terms. But the Upper Creeks were angered over this treaty and called it treason. They set fire to McIntosh's house and when he fled the flames, they shot him.

Most of the Lower Creeks, led by Roley McIntosh, traveled by boat to Indian Territory. The first group arrived at Fort Gibson in 1828. This was the first time a steamboat had ascended the Arkansas River that far. The Upper Creeks continued to resist the pressure from Democratic leaders such as President Andrew Jackson to move west.

But they finally were forced to sign a treaty agreeing to give up their Georgia lands. Ironically, the treaty they finally signed had much worse terms for them than the one McIntosh signed. The U.S. Army rounded up the Upper Creeks and moved them forcibly over the Trail of Tears to Indian Territory.

The Creek Nation in Indian Territory was bounded by the Verdigris and Arkansas Rivers on the North and the forks of the Canadian on the South. The Lower Creeks, who arrived first, settled in the North along the Arkansas and Verdigris and established the towns of Creek Agency, Koweta and Tulsey Town. The Upper Creeks came later and chose to live along the Canadian branches at North Fork Town and Okmulgee. Because of past animosities, tensions still existed between the two groups.

There was a desire among them, however, to try to reach a place of cooperation in their new lands. They agreed to hold an annual council at a place called High Springs. The hill near the springs became known as the Council Hill and the town that has that name is located near the springs and the meeting place. Each town would send a representative to the annual council meeting. As the Creeks worked together they began to prosper in their new towns.

Divisions repeatedly cropped up along the same Upper and Lower Creek lines. But each time conflict arose, the Creeks would again work to mend their divisions and find a way to work together. Today the Creek Nation works from a Council House in Okmulgee that was designed to represent the ancient mounds of their ancestors who surely had to work in cooperation to build them long, long ago.

Fountain Church Survived a Long History

In September of 1832, the Muskoke Baptist Church was organized as a part of the Ebenezer Mission, making the church one of the first established in Oklahoma. Ebenezer Mission had been a school in Georgia and when the Creeks removed to the Three Rivers area, John Davis and his wife, members of the Creek tribe, continued the school here.

In 1832, Rev. Isaac McCoy was commissioned by the federal government to survey the Cherokee Outlet and mark its boundaries. Having traveled in this area on previous occasions, he was familiar with the territory. He came to the Three Rivers region with his family and settled at Union Mission on the Grand River in what is Mayes County today.

Rev. McCoy, an ordained minister from Kentucky, had long been involved with mission work among various Native American tribes, most recently in Michigan. McCoy believed, like many others at that time, that separation between the white and Indian cultures was the best way to keep peace and so he had favored the establishment of Indian Territory. Some Native Americans shared this view, while others did not and this brought tension and conflict within the tribes themselves.

Rev. McCoy met John Davis and began working with him at Ebenezer Mission. For a time, the little church met in homes around Three Forks. Then in 1833, the first meeting house for the church was built about 15 miles west of Fort Gibson. This first building was a log structure according to early accounts. The first church members included Mr. and Mrs. Davis, the pastor Rev. David Lewis and his wife who were white and three African Americans named Quash, Bob and Ned.

Lewis left this work in 1834 and a new pastor named David Rollin arrived in Indian Territory. Rev. Rollin found the church somewhat disorganized, but it had grown to include six white members, twenty-two Indian members and fifty-four black members. Unfortunately, the integrated nature of the church caused opposition to it.

Complaints were made to the Creek leadership that the missionaries at Ebenezer were preaching against slavery. They also were allowing African Americans, who were most likely slaves, to hold leadership positions in the church. In addition to these charges, some Creek leaders felt that the mission was pulling Creeks away from their traditional ways.

All of these complaints resulted in the Creek chief Roley McIntosh asking the Creek agent to remove all white missionaries from the Nation, which the agent did. However supporters of Rev. Rollin intervened on his behalf and he was exonerated of any wrongdoing and allowed to return.

The work of the mission went forward until the Civil War when everything in Indian Territory was disrupted. Following the war, the church was reorganized and renamed Fountain Church because there was a spring on the church grounds.

Minutes from the Creek Freedmen's Baptist Association of 1892 indicate that Fountain Church was organized in 1867. The Oklahoma Baptist Convention erected a marker on Highway 69 in 1977 to commemorate the fact that Fountain Church is the successor of Ebenezer Mission and is the oldest Baptist church in Oklahoma.

The Largest Military Expedition in Indian Territory Was a Rescue Mission

In early summer of 1834, a Texas man named Judge Martin left his home on the Red River and came into Indian Territory on a hunting expedition. He brought his sons and two slaves with him and they made camp near the Washita River. The camp was attacked by Comanches and only one of Martin's sons survived. He was taken captive by the war party.

When word reached Fort Gibson that the young boy, Matthew Martin, was alive and being held by the Comanches, a military expedition was launched from the fort to rescue the boy. It would become known as the Dragoon Expedition and was the largest military undertaking in Indian Territory history.

The Dragoons were a cavalry unit commanded by General Henry Leavenworth. They had recently been organized and they made an impressive picture as they rode out of Fort Gibson in June of 1834. Hundreds of soldiers both on foot and horseback made their way southwestward with a long train of supply wagons and pack animals.

Each company in the Dragoons had its own color of horse, specially matched. One company had all black horses; the other five had bays, whites, sorrels, grays and cream colored horses.

Many well-known military figures were a part of the expedition. In addition to Gen. Leavenworth, Henry Dodge, Stephen Kearny, Nathan Boone and Jefferson Davis made up the ranks of the Dragoons. The famous western artist George Catlin also accompanied the cavalry and recorded the event in his paintings.

The Dragoons moved as rapidly as possible across Indian Territory. The expedition proved difficult and costly in terms of the soldiers' lives. Because of the urgent pace in the oppressive July heat and poor drinking water, many sickened and died along the route, including General Leavenworth.

The soldiers literally had to cut a road across unsettled wilderness as they made their way to the Washita River. The trail they cut later was known as an alternate part of the Texas Road.

After crossing the Washita, they moved westward toward the Wichita Mountains to arrive at a large Wichita village. Here Colonel Dodge, who had assumed command after Leavenworth fell ill, met with Wichita, Kiowa and Comanche leaders.

An exchange of captives was made. The Dragoons had brought with them two Kiowa girls who had been taken captive by the Osage. The girls were exchanged for young Matthew Martin.

The Kiowas were greatly pleased with the return of the two girls and the exchange created a sense of goodwill between the soldiers and the Plains tribes. Matthew Martin accompanied the Dragoons back to Fort Gibson and then was returned to his grateful mother in Texas.

Tulasi Gave Birth to Tulsa

The removal of the Creek Nation from Alabama, Florida and Georgia covered a span of several years. The first of several groups arrived in 1828 but migrations continued through the 1830s. Following their traditional settlement patterns, each of the migrating groups chose a location along the rivers within the boundaries of their new nation in Indian Territory.

In 1836 a group of Lochapoka (Turtle Clan) Creeks reached a location on the Arkansas River and chose to re-establish their ceremonial fire under a large oak tree there. This tree became known as the Council Oak, an easily recognized landmark where they would meet for councils, ceremonies and dances. The Council Oak became the gathering place for Tulasi, a Muscogee word meaning "old town."

For the Creeks a "town" was not necessarily a municipality with buildings, streets and some form of government. A "town" was a political and social organization to which its members belonged. Tulasi Town then existed as a gathering location for many years without being a physical community.

In 1846, Creek leader Lewis Perryman settled near the Council Oak and established a log trading post. This helped establish Tulsey Town, as it was called then, as a commercial center. Other Creeks set up farms and ranches in the vicinity and they prospered until the devastation of the Civil War. Most Creek citizens fled the territory and spent the war years as refugees. Homes and ranches were destroyed; livestock fed the armies of both the North and the South.

Following the war, Creeks returned and slowly rebuilt their homes. True communities began to develop as well. The ranch of Josiah Perryman, son of Lewis, became the location of Tulsa's first post office not far from the Arkansas River on the east bank. It later moved to the ranch of George Perryman, further north and closer to what would become downtown Tulsa.

Tulsa received rail service in 1882 when the Atlantic and Pacific Railroad built a spur down into the cattle ranching area. At the time, Tulsa had a population of about 200. As in every other town it touched, the railroad brought non-Indians into the region.

Two brothers, James and Harry Hall set up the first permanent store near the end of the rail line. James Hall became the town's biggest booster and helped to lay out its streets, form its first government, helped to build its first church and school and serve as postmaster.

That first church and school were a part of the Presbyterian Mission and were located near Fourth and Boston in 1884. When Tulsa incorporated and formed a city government in 1898, the school became its first public education facility.

The Glenn Pool oil strike in 1905 changed the course of Tulsa's history. As the closest community with rail service, Tulsa became the focal point for oil industry development and as Oklahoma became a state, Tulsa became its oil capital.

Early Muskogee Was Called Creek Agency

Besides Fort Gibson, Salina and Webbers Falls, one of the earliest settlements in the vicinity of the Three Rivers was a town called Creek Agency. This community served as the precursor to Muskogee and occupied several locations in its history.

Around 1828, A.P. Chouteau sold his trading post on the east bank of the Verdigris River near present day Okay to David Brearley, the newly appointed Creek agent. Brearley had been put in charge of overseeing the Creek removal from their lands in the southeastern United States to Indian Territory.

The first Creek emigrants arrived at this site in February 1828, on the steamboat *Facility*. Over the next few years, several more steamboats arrived carrying the Creeks to their new home. In New Orleans, steamship companies began advertising Creek Agency as one of their destination points west of the Mississippi.

In 1833, a severe flood wiped out the Agency building and most of the little community of trading posts and cabins located at Three Forks. At this time, Creek Agency moved further west to the property of Creek Chief Chilly McIntosh. It was here that Creek Agency gained a post office in 1843. From this location, the Creek Agency made another move around 1851 to the south side of the Arkansas River at the base of Fern Mountain. Early fur traders had already been established in this area for a number of years.

A map sketched by a very early settler named T.F. Meagher shows the Creek Agency community just before Muskogee came into being. The Creek Agency was in the center of a group of homes and businesses and the Creek courthouse was located southeast of the agency. The per capita payments by the government to the Creeks were made at the courthouse. A Creek schoolhouse sat to the northeast.

Across the road from the Agency building was the store of George Stidham for whom the town of Stidham was named. Later James A. Patterson operated his mercantile in this same building. The Parkinson store was northeast of the agency building and a nearby group of cabins made up Aunt Sarah's Boarding House, most probably where the Indians stayed when visiting the Agency or coming to trade their furs. A blacksmith shop was another business located nearby.

T.F. Meagher's home was due north of the agency and a number of other cabins were scattered throughout the vicinity. One cabin where Charles Foster lived was known as the Gingerbread Cabin because his wife Nancy Lott baked and sold gingerbread here. Rev. John Bemo, a Seminole preacher had a large homestead nearby.

According to Meagher's notations on his map a Civil War battle between Confederate Creek and Cherokee forces and Union Creek, Cherokee and Osage forces occurred near the Agency. He also marked the location of graves of Civil War soldiers, most likely those who were killed in this battle. The Wealaka Road, Tullahassee Road and Hitchita Trail all passed near the Agency.

Creek Agency continued as a town until the Missouri, Kansas & Texas Railroad built through the area in 1872. Then the businesses and eventually the agency itself moved into the new town of Muskogee to be closer to the rail line, and the town of Creek Agency eventually ceased to exist.

Coodey Played Major Role in Cherokee Politics

Across the Arkansas River from where Muskogee's OG&E Power Plant is now located, a small Cherokee community developed around the homestead of William Shorey Coodey. He was a prominent Cherokee leader for whom the nearby creek was named. This community was called Frozen Rock and an old cemetery is one of the few reminders of the existence of the town that developed before the Civil War.

William Coodey was the son of Jane Ross Coodey who was the oldest sister of Cherokee chief John Ross. He was born in Chattanooga, Tennessee around 1806 and received his education there. He was elected secretary of the Cherokee delegation that traveled to Washington, D.C. in 1830 with another prominent Cherokee citizen named Sam Houston. Coodey was an active leader in the Cherokee Nation for all of his life.

In 1834, the Coodey family removed from Tennessee to Indian Territory. By 1838, they had built a large double log cabin on the high western bank of the Arkansas River at Frozen Rock. It was such a well-built home that Carolyn Thomas Foreman wrote it was still standing some 85 years later.

To this home many influential members of the Cherokee Nation would gather to discuss the important political happenings of the day. The home was one of the most refined in Indian Territory with the finest furnishings imported from the states. They were brought by steamboat to a landing at Frozen Rock. Steamboats would frequently make a stop here before proceeding to Fort Gibson or Creek Agency.

The site of Frozen Rock had earlier been a Seminole campsite when members of that nation first arrived in Indian Territory. They landed by steamboat at Fort Gibson and resided near the fort until they were eventually settled on Creek-held land further to the west. Coodey's daughter Ella later recalled finding blue beads left from the Seminole camp when she would play in the dirt around the foundation of the house.

The Coodey home was run in the manner of a Southern plantation and the Coodeys did hold slaves. One African American slave was named Rabbit and once freed by Coodey he maintained the ford across the river at Frozen Rock and it became known as Rabbit's Ford. It was at this ford that Union troops from Fort Gibson crossed the Arkansas River to attack and destroy the Confederate Fort Davis where it was located north of the present campus of Bacone College.

When William Coodey and his family arrived in Indian Territory, tensions were still very high between the Western and Eastern factions of the Cherokees. Coodey helped to write the Act of Union between these two factions and also was the author of the Cherokee Constitution. Nearly every year, Coodey would travel with a Cherokee delegation to Washington to meet with government officials on matters pertaining to the nation.

Coodey died in Washington in April 1849 at the age of forty-three. He was buried at the Congressional Cemetery. The *Washington Union* newspaper commended him at his death as "a citizen of the Cherokee Nation long and favorably known to the government and to the citizens of Washington as an able and faithful representative of the Cherokee people."

Cherokee Payment Saved From River Disaster

Travel by steamboat up the Arkansas River was a precarious business in the early days of river navigation. Besides the ever present danger of hitting "snags" – submerged logs and other debris – boiler explosions and fires were also a hazard to the steam-powered boats. Few steamboats survived more than four or five years of service between New Orleans and Three Forks.

One such steamboat was named the *Cherokee* which plied the rivers between New Orleans and Fort Gibson and the Creek Agency. In December of 1840, the *Cherokee* carried as a passenger Captain William Armstrong, the Superintendent of Indian Affairs for the western tribes. Armstrong had traveled to New Orleans to secure a payment for the Cherokees in accordance with their treaty with the federal government. The payment of over $100,000 was to be made at Fort Gibson.

The paper money making up the bulk of the payment was sealed in watertight kegs. An additional amount in gold and silver coins was locked in two strongboxes and kept in the clerk's office.

After the steamboat had passed Little Rock and was 60 miles upriver of that town, the *Cherokee*'s boiler exploded. Tragically some 15 crew and passengers were killed and several others were wounded. The boat was torn apart by the explosion and within an hour sank in the Arkansas River.

Captain Armstrong reported to his supervisor that the box of gold was blown onto shore, split open and the coins were spilled about. Armstrong estimated about $90 worth of coins were lost. The box of silver coin, dimes and "half-dimes," was blown onto the bow of the boat and virtually disintegrated. Armstrong scrambled to retrieve all the change he could and estimated he saved all but about $50.

The kegs holding the paper money fell to a lower deck of the boat, but because they had been secured with iron hoops they did not break apart. None of the paper money was lost. Armstrong, however, was forced to wait several days at the site of the explosion, guarding the money. It was a great relief to him when another steamboat arrived to carry the retrieved funds on to Fort Gibson where they were distributed to the Cherokees gathered there.

Such tragic and frightening incidents were quite common in the days of steamboat travel. The depths of the Arkansas River may still be littered with the remains of vessels that plied its waters in earlier times.

Stidham Had Long Influence in Creek Nation

George W. Stidham left a lasting mark on the Creek Nation in Indian Territory by his many years of service to his people. Born to a Scotch-Irish father and Creek mother in Alabama in 1817, Stidham did not learn to speak English until he was twenty years old. His opportunities for education were limited, but he worked to educate himself.

Around 1837, Stidham moved to the Creek Nation in Indian Territory, settling in the Choska Bottom area near Haskell. He had become proficient enough in English that one of his first jobs for the tribe was acting as an interpreter for the Creek Agent. Shortly, Stidham was sent to Washington to represent the Creeks there. It would be the first of more than fifteen trips to Washington that Stidham would take during his lifetime of working for the Creek Nation.

Stidham went into the mercantile business in the Creek Agency community near Fern Mountain and was working in this capacity at the outbreak of the Civil War.

Along with most of the tribe, Stidham and his family were forced to flee the Territory for the duration of the War. They spent that time living near Texarkana.

Returning to his business at Creek Agency, Stidham worked there for a time before selling his firm to James Parkinson. George Stidham then concentrated his efforts in agriculture and is said to have been the first farmer in Indian Territory to plant wheat and to utilize a threshing machine. He also encouraged the planting of this crop among his neighbors.

For nearly all of his adult life George Stidham was involved in the politics of his tribe. He represented his tribal town of Hitchetee in the House of Warriors for a number of years and also served several terms as a judge. At the time of his death in 1891, Stidham was Chief Justice for the Creek Nation.

George Stidham also had the distinction of being a charter member of the first Masonic Lodge organized in Indian Territory and at his death was a Royal Arch Mason. The town of Stidham in McIntosh County was named for this leader among the Creeks who spent his life working for the betterment of his people.

Early Missionary Was Master Linguist

Ann Eliza Worcester was the daughter of Samuel and Ann Worcester who were serving as missionaries to the Cherokees at Brainerd Mission in Tennessee when she was born in 1826. It was at Brainerd that Ann Eliza first developed a passion for teaching and concern for Native Americans. She, with the Cherokees, made the difficult journey to Indian Territory with her parents when she was just nine years old. The Worcesters continued their work at a new mission at Park Hill near Tahlequah.

Ann Eliza attended the school at Park Hill that her father established. This school would later develop into the Cherokee Female Seminary. The Worcesters were firm believers in education, including for women. Ann Eliza was sent to live with an uncle in Vermont when she was fifteen so that she might pursue a college education at St. Johnsbury Academy.

While most young ladies of that day studied the arts Ann Eliza studied Greek and Latin, the languages of science. A professor at the school recognized her gift for language and persuaded Ann Eliza's uncle to allow her to pursue this unusual course of study for a young woman.

Ann Eliza returned to Park Hill in 1846 and began work there as a teacher. Though she was a candidate for a master's degree, she felt she was needed at the mission in Indian Territory.

A few years later, she attended a missions conference in Arkansas with her father and there met another young missionary named William Robertson. He was just beginning to work among the Creeks at the Tullahassee Mission. The two young teachers began a courtship and William would often ride his horse over to Park Hill to visit Ann Eliza there. In 1850 William and Ann Eliza married and she became his assistant at Tullahassee.

Because she struggled with poor health, Ann Eliza was often bedridden at the mission. Her older daughters, Augusta and Alice, learned at a very young age to shoulder the responsibility of caring for their younger siblings and in helping run the mission. Altogether Ann Eliza bore seven children, but three died at young ages.

Despite her illness, Ann Eliza worked even from her bed. Her gift for languages made her a capable translator and the hours she spent resting were also spent translating the Bible, hymns, and school primers into the Muscogee language.

Ann Eliza used her adversity as an opportunity and for the remainder of her life she was faithfully working on a translation. In early city directories, Ann Eliza Robertson's occupation was listed as "translator." In her lifetime, she translated the entire New Testament from Greek into Muscogee.

Her work earned her the respect of the mission community. In 1892, she was awarded an honorary doctorate from the University of Wooster in Ohio. She was the first woman in the United States to receive such an honor.

In later years, Ann Eliza lived with her daughter Alice in Muskogee where she continued her translation work and served as professor emeritus for Henry Kendall College. She was not able to lecture at the college, but was always willing to tutor young students who needed her assistance. Always a missionary at heart, Ann Eliza died at age 79 in 1905 and was working on the fifth revision of her New Testament translation at the time of her death.

5

Indian Territory

Tribal Neutrality Proved Impossible in the Civil War

When one by one the southern states began to secede from the Union in 1861, the Five Civilized Tribes of Indian Territory found themselves under increasing pressure to join the Confederate cause. With Confederate states on the east and south and only Kansas on the north siding with the Union, Indian Territory was caught in a vice. Aligning with the South seemed like the expedient thing to do.

Yet many members of the tribes wanted to remain neutral and take no part in "the white man's war." They argued that the Five Tribes should simply stay out of the conflict and then negotiate with whoever was left standing. But their attempt at a neutral stance proved almost impossible to maintain.

Tribal leaders such as Cherokee chief John Ross, argued for neutrality, hoping to maintain the fragile unity his tribe had found after years of conflict over removal. If he could urge his nation to remain neutral, perhaps they could avoid being pulled back into the factionalism that had plagued them so long. Beside this, the federal government held a large amount of money in trust for the Cherokees. To sign a treaty with the Confederacy could mean a forfeiture of these funds.

But many Cherokees, led by men such as Stand Waite, strongly sided with the Confederacy and began forming military regiments to involve themselves in the war. Ross felt increasing pressure to sign an alliance treaty with the South and when the Union pulled all federal troops out of Indian Territory to help with the war effort back east, Ross felt he had but one choice. He chose the South.

John Ross would later write that he felt like a man standing alone on a spot of ground while flood waters rose around him. If a log were to drift by him, should he not seize it in order to save his life? For Ross, the alliance treaty was his grasp at the best opportunity for saving the unity of his tribe. With all U.S. authority gone from the Territory, Confederate forces all around, and the other Five Tribes joining the South, Ross made the decision he would later regret.

When federal troops returned to Indian Territory in 1862 and occupied the Cherokee capital of Tahlequah, Ross was arrested and taken to Washington. By this time, he had grown disenchanted with the Confederacy which had proved no more inclined to keep its treaty obligations than the U.S. government. Factionalism had returned to the Cherokees despite his efforts to avoid them.

When Ross met with President Abraham Lincoln after his arrest, he explained his motives for joining with the South and pledged a return to the Union. He would hold this position until his death only a few years later. In the end, the Cherokees, like the other Five Tribes, suffered through the "white man's war" in part because their desire for neutrality had proved impossible.

Fort Blunt Named for Honey Springs Commander

Shortly after Confederate forces fired upon Fort Sumter in South Carolina, commencing the American Civil War, there was rush among Union sympathizers to raise military forces. In Kansas, a physician named James G. Blunt was among the first to volunteer. He had practiced medicine in Greeley, Kansas for several years and was a staunch abolitionist.

He joined the Third Kansas Regiment and was given the rank of Lt. Colonel. This regiment was sent to Fort Scott, Kansas to defend it against Confederate troops under General Sterling Price. After spending several months in pursuit of Price throughout Kansas and Missouri, Blunt was made a Brigadier General and placed in command of Fort Leavenworth.

Blunt was responsible for organizing regiments of Creek, Cherokee and Seminole refugees who had fled Indian Territory to Kansas at the outbreak of hostilities. Utilizing these troops, Blunt sent forces into Indian Territory as far as Tahlequah in 1862, but they returned to Fort Scott, Kansas rather than remain in the Territory.

Blunt then left Fort Leavenworth and personally assumed command of the Indian troops. He would later write of them that they remained on active duty till the end of the war and "did excellent service for the Union cause." Blunt would lead his troops to battles throughout Missouri and Arkansas, including the well-known clashes at Pea Ridge and Prairie Grove.

By 1863, Blunt had also added to his command one of the first African American regiments to fight in the Civil War – the First Kansas Colored Infantry. With success in the Arkansas battles, Blunt was determined to secure Indian Territory for the Union. He ordered a subordinate, Colonel William Phillips, to occupy Fort Gibson. Blunt would join Phillips there with additional troops on July 11, 1863.

By this time, General Blunt's reputation as a bold and disciplined fighter had been well established. Upon his arrival at Fort Gibson, its name was changed to Fort Blunt, though it only was referred to by this name for a brief time.

Blunt learned that Confederate troops were massing at a supply depot called Honey Springs and more reinforcements were expected to arrive from Arkansas. Their intent was to attack Fort Gibson. But as he had done on several other occasions, Blunt decided to strike first before the additional troops could arrive.

Leaving Fort Gibson on July 16, Blunt's forces made the 20-mile march to Honey Springs overnight. They engaged the Confederate troops under General Douglas Cooper at a point where the Texas Road crossed Elk Creek. With the First Kansas Colored Infantry holding the center of the Union line, the Confederate forces were routed and forced to retreat. Because of the Union victory at Honey Springs, Fort Gibson, or Fort Blunt, was never again seriously threatened by Southern troops for the remainder of the Civil War.

Three Forks Was Crossroads for Travelers

Before the railroad crossed through Indian Territory in 1871 and 1872, travelers through this frontier area depended upon horses or teams of mules and oxen for transportation. From this, it might seem that travel would have been sparse. But that was not the case. Long before the historic highways such as Route 69 were laid across Oklahoma, this area was one of the crossroads of the American West.

Indian trails were first to leave their mark upon the land, running from the Three Rivers juncture to trade centers such as St. Louis, Santa Fe and Natchitoches, Louisiana. Then the military roads were built along these trails to connect Fort Smith, Fort Gibson and Fort Riley, Kansas.

By the 1830s and 1840s, emigrants were traveling through the Three Rivers area heading to Texas for land or to California and Colorado for gold. The Texas Road and the California Trail crossed each other in the Three Rivers region. Early visitors recorded in their journals that on some days hundreds of oxen-drawn wagons could be seen on these roads. Ruts from the iron-rimmed wheels of these wagons left deep scars on the land and some were still visible a hundred years later.

Following the devastation of the Civil War, the roads were rebuilt and travel resumed. Now transit and stage companies competed for the traffic along the roads. The Overland Transit Company hauled freight from Texas to wherever the railroad terminated. The Butterfield Overland Mail had a government contract to haul the mail and military supplies.

The El Paso Stage Line ran from Baxter Springs, Kansas through the Three Forks, and on to other points such as Fort Smith, before crossing the Red River at Colbert's Ferry and continuing on to El Paso, Texas. The stage carried both passengers and freight.

By the 1870s the El Paso Stage was running a regular route from Fort Smith to the new railroad town of Muskogee. This is where Fort Smith residents would catch the train bound for St. Louis or points further east. In 1872, the stage line advertised in the Fort Smith newspaper that it would offer a fine four-horse stage leaving at 6:30 a.m.

each Monday, Wednesday and Friday and arriving at Muscogee Station by midnight. This nearly 18-hour journey, however, proved too strenuous for passengers so the arrival time was pushed back to 11:00 a.m. the next day.

Muskogee also saw passenger stages leaving for Okmulgee, Wewoka, Sac and Fox Agency, Shawneetown and Kickapoo each Monday and Thursday and returning on Wednesday and Saturday. Students attending the Cherokee Seminaries at Park Hill could take the stage to and from school each weekend.

Both the freighters and stage lines usually traveled with some type of armed guard to ensure the safety of the passengers and to protect against thievery. Gangs of outlaws preyed upon the transit lines and it was their frequent complaints to the government that helped to bring a federal court and federal marshals to Muskogee.

At times the Three Rivers region was crowded with folks all headed for someplace else. For many years this area was a "just passing through" location on the map except for the Five Civilized Tribes. But without fail, those who kept a record of their journey through the Three Rivers region always commented on the beauty of this land.

Early Ferries Were Essential to Frontier Travel

Crossing the vast American frontier was a challenge for those hardy pioneers who ventured westward. Out here putting a bridge across a small creek or stream might be a matter of cutting a couple of trees long enough to span the water and nailing spaced boards along their length. But bridges over rivers such as the Arkansas, Grand and Verdigris took more equipment, manpower and engineering than existed in the early days of Oklahoma's settlement.

The only way to get across the rivers was to ford them – to wade into the water and hope to be able to make it to the other side. Fording the rivers in the Three Rivers area could be difficult, even dangerous, and was not for the faint of heart. If the river level was too high, even the most intrepid traveler could not get across. Quicksand was not unheard of and rapid currents could pull even a team of horses down.

As more and more people began to move through or settle in the Three Rivers area, the need for accessible river crossings increased. And a few enterprising individuals saw a business opportunity in this need. They started ferry operations along the rivers at natural fording spots. Often a small community had already developed around these locations, serving the needs of area residents and travelers who would come there to cross the river.

One of the earliest ferries in operation was the Nivens Ferry that crossed the Arkansas River just south of its juncture with the Grand River. Travelers on the military road to and from Fort Gibson would use this ferry as would settlers heading south on the Texas Road.

Two other ferries on the Arkansas were the Smith Ferry and Drew's Ferry located to the south and north of the Nivens Ferry respectively on branches of the Texas Road which brought a surprising amount of traffic through the region. Ferry operators charged a fee to carry individuals, their horses, oxen and wagons across the river. At busy crossings, a ferry operator could make a good living providing such transportation.

Some travelers grumbled about the fee, but most recognized that it was a service they needed and it was better than risking their lives or possessions to turbulent water or hidden quicksand. Ferries also allowed travelers to cross the river regardless of the water level. The only problem with the ferries was that when they were busy, people would have to line up at the crossing and wait their turn to get across.

At Webbers Falls, a ferry was begun by a Cherokee doctor named William Campbell. He operated two ferries – a steam ferry when the river level was high and a cable ferry when the water was low.

Campbell started his ferry out of necessity. His home was located at the river and he would often have complete strangers stranded and camped in his yard or staying in his house because the river level was too high for them to cross.

Campbell's ferry helped establish a town on the other side of the river opposite Webbers Falls. At first it was called Illinois Station, then the town was called Campbell. The town later changed its name to Gore in honor of Senator Thomas P. Gore.

Ferries continued in operation well after statehood in Oklahoma. By the 1920s with the development of the Jefferson Highway, a push for paved roads led finally to the building of bridges over the rivers. Ferries and fords then became a thing of the past over the waters of the Three Rivers area.

Government Payments Brought Needed Currency to Territory

In its dealings with the Five Civilized Tribes, the federal government often included payments of large amounts of cash for various reasons. The tribes were compensated in cash for the lands they gave up in the southeastern United States. Other payments were made to individuals who were orphaned by the death of their parents in the removals, to these who suffered property losses during the Civil War or to those who suffered crop losses during severe droughts in Indian Territory.

Making these payments was always a major event in the Indian Nations. Simply transporting the large amounts of cash, sometimes in the hundreds of thousands of dollars, took a great deal of security measures. For payments made to the Creeks or Cherokees, troops at Fort Gibson were usually part of the security detail.

The money would often be sent by train to the Union Agency in Muskogee and from there it would be distributed to the tribes. Since the tribes all had capitals some distance from Muskogee, transporting the funds to their capital for disbursement to their own members would usually involve the protection of their lighthorsemen.

When George Washington Grayson was elected Creek national treasurer in 1869, one of his first responsibilities was to receive an annuity payment of $100,000 from the government. He traveled to Creek Agency to pick up the payment, well aware of the dangers that would be involved in transporting it on to Okmulgee, the Creek capital.

Grayson happened to see Johnson Kennard, a lighthorseman, among the crowd gathered at the agency. Privately he asked Kennard for an escort to Okmulgee.

After dark, the two men casually rode out of town. When out of sight of the village, they spurred their horses to a quicker pace to cross the 40 miles of prairie from Fern Mountain to Okmulgee. Though they took a rest stop along the way to catch a few hours sleep, they were able to reach the Creek capital without incident.

Since the tribes themselves did not issue any type of currency, Indian Territory was often cash poor. The tribes and some merchants would offer warrants or scrip to individuals and these circulated like money. When an annuity payment was due to arrive in Indian Territory, merchants were more ready to extend credit, knowing their tribal customers would soon have true cash to pay their bills.

An almost carnival-like atmosphere would develop at the site where a payment was to be made. Tribal members would arrive in a holiday mood and so would creditors who expected to collect on sometimes long-standing debts. Unfortunately, after the recipients of the annuity payment finished paying off their debts, they were often cash poor once again. But the influx of cash was at least for a brief time a much-needed stimulus to the Indian Territory economy.

Thanksgiving at Creek Agency Fondly Remembered

Thanksgiving is associated with the *Mayflower* Pilgrims who celebrated with their Native American neighbors in New England. Following that first Thanksgiving, the holiday was celebrated sporadically, but was not an official national holiday until Abraham Lincoln set aside the fourth Thursday in November for giving thanks.

Even in Indian Territory, Thanksgiving was being celebrated just following the Civil War. In 1867, Colonel W.H. Garrett, the U.S. agent to the Creek Nation, issued an invitation to Thanksgiving dinner to the Robertson family, who served at the Tullahassee Mission across the Arkansas River. The Creek Agency and the little settlement around it was then located on the south side of the Arkansas near Fern Mountain.

The Robertson family set out early that Thursday morning, despite signs of a storm brewing on the horizon. They had to ford the Arkansas, but their one horse, Old Jim, pulled their little wagon safely across. William and Ann Eliza Robertson and their children Alice, Grace and Samuel arrived at the Garrett home which was a spacious log cabin with stone chimneys at each end. It was the

Robertsons' first visit to the Creek Agency since it had located near Fern Mountain following the war.

The missionary family was greeted by Colonel and Mrs. Garrett and their son, daughter-in-law and baby granddaughter. They were ushered into the warm house decorated with boughs of scarlet berries and mistletoe. The children were offered apples and nuts to enjoy before the big Thanksgiving feast was served.

The meal had been prepared by Aunt Sarah Davis, an African Creek woman who ran an inn and eatery at the Creek Agency community. Sarah was known to be one of the best cooks in the Creek Nation and her turkey with rice stuffing was a specialty. The Robertson children had to remind themselves to eat slowly and mind their manners as their mother had instructed them.

Before the meal was completed the storm that had threatened all morning broke in a great gust of wind and rain. The rain changed to sleet and eventually snow so the Robertsons were invited to spend the night rather than try to return home in such weather. The soft drifting snow at the end of the day only served to make in all the more memorable for Alice Robertson who recalled it fondly many years later.

First Bridges Were Built for the Railroad

In the spring of 1871, the Missouri, Kansas & Texas Railroad (the Katy) won the right to cross Indian Territory by being the first rail line to reach the border with the Cherokee Nation. The railroad's managers believed they could cross quickly through the Indian nations to reach the cattle lands of Texas.

But they underestimated the difficulties of crossing what was still a sparsely populated land. First the railroad workers were hampered by early spring rains that turned the prairie to mud. Then mosquitoes nearly drove them crazy as they worked through swampy bottomlands. By June 1871, they had reached Pryor Creek, just 50 miles from the Kansas border with another 50 miles to go before reaching Fort Gibson.

Another hindrance was the open hostility many Cherokees felt toward the railroad. Individual Indians fenced off the best timberlands, forcing the railroad to negotiate with dozens of Cherokees for railroad ties instead of buying them through the Cherokee national council. So frustrating was the lack of cooperation by the Cherokees, the Katy managers decided to change the course of the railroad. Instead of following the Texas Road into Fort Gibson, the rail line would follow the road's western fork so that it would enter the Creek Nation as soon as possible.

By the end of July, the line had advanced only ten miles to Chouteau's Creek and it was late August before it passed Flat Rock Creek in present-day Wagoner County. When the workers arrive at the Verdigris River, the railroad established a depot that gained the name Gibson Station because a supply road was built from it to Fort Gibson. Passenger service from Gibson Station began in September 1871.

When the rail line reached the Three Rivers area, two river bridges had to be built – first over the Verdigris and then three and a half miles further south over the Arkansas. The railroad supervisor expected to have the bridge over the Verdigris completed by September 15 and over the Arkansas by October 1. Again, these deadlines proved unreachable.

Because the ironwork had to be shipped in from the American Bridge Company in Chicago, the three spans of the Verdigris bridge were not in place until October 1. On that fateful day, the center span collapsed, killing several workers and injuring many more. A new span would have to be shipped in from Chicago. But on October 8, the Great

Chicago Fire broke out and the American Bridge Company had to delay all its shipments.

Work resumed after this delay and the Verdigris bridge was completed by the end of October. The tracklayers, who normally could lay a mile of track a day, took eleven days to cross the three and half miles to the Arkansas. They were delayed this time by heavy rains and a jungle of river cane. Then on November 17, a heavy rainfall flooded the Arkansas and washed out the framework for its bridge. The workers had to start over once again.

By December 7, the bridge was completed and ready for track to be laid across it to the site of old Fort Davis. This was the original site chosen for a large depot, but the terrain proved too uneven. So the tracklayers slogged through more rain, mud and cane to a site three miles further south. Here the depot would be built and named Muscogee Station in honor of the Creek tribe.

In a ceremony to celebrate finally reaching this milestone, the first steam engine crossed the Katy's Arkansas River bridge on Christmas Day 1871. This steam locomotive was called a "General Grant" and the trial run across the bridge must have been a great satisfaction to the weary workers who had toiled for many months to finally reach the heart of Indian Territory.

Family Left Mark on Muskogee

Joseph Sondheimer, a Jewish immigrant from Bavaria, arrived in America in 1852 at the age of 12. He had come to the "land of promise" alone, but quickly located family friends in Baltimore and moved in with them. He learned the mercantile trade and tramped about the Midwest as a peddler. He settled in St. Louis just before the Civil War broke out.

In 1866, Sondheimer secured a trade permit from the Secretary of the Interior to do business in Indian Territory. Traveling on a large white horse, Sondheimer developed a trade circuit throughout the territory, purchasing furs and hides for cash. He carried the gold coin in his saddlebag and remarkably, at a time when outlaws roamed freely, the fur trader was never once robbed.

Eventually Sondheimer built several warehouses along the Texas Road where he would store the furs he bought until he could ship them back east. He had plants at Creek Agency and Fort Davis as well as Wagoner and Muskogee.

In 1872, Sondheimer requested permission to settle in Indian Territory and bring his family there from St. Louis. He planned to build a home near the old Fort Davis site north of Muskogee because the Missouri, Kansas and Texas Railroad had plans to locate a depot here. When the depot was located further south and Muskogee was born, Sondheimer moved his family to this new town instead.

Sondheimer had fur plants at both ends of Second Street in Muskogee – one near Fondulac where Arrowhead Mall stands today and one at Okmulgee where the Federal Building is now located. Sondheimer's business continued in Muskogee until 1942, carried on by his sons Alexander and Samuel.

The Sondheimers were very involved in Muskogee's civic activities and were great supporters of the town. Joseph supported the Beth Ahaba Congregation and a stained glass window in the Temple was inlaid with his name and date of death. Samuel served on the Board of Directors of the First National Bank.

But it was Alexander Sondheimer who perhaps left the most lasting legacy to Muskogee. He and his wife Eudora were tragically killed in an accident while traveling in Europe in 1923. In their estate, they generously bequeathed funds to several Muskogee institutions including the YMCA, the YWCA, the Boy Scouts, United Charities (an early version of the United Way), the Presbyterian Church (her congregation) and Beth Ahaba (his congregation).

The most interesting bequest, however, was one to the Masons. The will set aside a sum of money for a Masonic pilgrimage to Pikes Peak to be made in 1998. Joseph Sondheimer had been Indian Territory's only citizen to make a similar trek to Pikes Peak with the Masons in 1898.

Cattle Production Has Always Been a Strong Area Industry

During earlier days, raising cattle was often the most profitable form of agriculture in this area. This was partly due to the peculiarities of land ownership in Indian Territory. Members of the tribes could use large tracts of land or could rent them out to stock raisers.

The prairie grasslands of the Three Rivers area were well suited to fattening cattle brought up from Texas. Hogs and sheep were also widely raised on tribal lands. Except for the rich river bottomlands, much of the prairie had a layer of sandstone beneath the topsoil. This made the region better suited for grazing cattle than for cultivating crops.

Every spring, great herds of cattle were shipped or driven in from Texas along the Texas Road. This route was also called the Shawnee Cattle Trail. Cowboys would drive the Texas longhorns northward in the spring. Muskogee was a sight to be seen when the herds would blow into town after weeks on the long, dusty trail. These cattle were fattened here all during the summer, and then shipped to northern markets in the fall. They arrived thin and weak and shipped out fat and strong after a summer of grazing on the rich prairie grasses.

H.B. Spaulding, for whom Spaulding Park in Muskogee is named, was one such stock raiser who profited greatly from the tribal system of land use. He married a Creek woman, which gave him access to Creek land. His ranch encompassed nearly 40 thousand acres between Muskogee and Checotah. His cattle herd numbered each year between 16 and 20 thousand head in the late 1890s.

F.B. Severs, a merchant and entrepreneur who built the Severs Hotel in downtown Muskogee, was another stockman who made his fortune in cattle. Though he was white, he had been adopted by the Creek Nation and could use tribal land. His ranch in the 1880s was so large it stretched from the outskirts of Muskogee all the way to Okmulgee. Enclosed by a minimum of wire fencing, thousands of head of cattle and an equal number of hogs roamed this vast ranch.

Another rancher was C.W. Turner whose 50 thousand acres lay to the south and west of Muskogee. Here ten thousand head of cattle were raised annually. Turner, with his partner, D.H. Middleton, also maintained feed lots north of the city of Muskogee where herds were fattened through the winter before being shipped to northern markets on the M-K-T Railroad. Turner and Middleton also cultivated nearly 900 acres on their ranch.

In the region that would become Tulsa, the George Perryman ranch occupied a vast area in the 1870s. Running from the Arkansas River to what is today Broken Arrow, this ranch was the largest in the area. It also raised thousands of head of cattle and made the Perryman family quite prosperous.

Each of these ranches provided employment for around twenty ranch hands throughout the year.

The fall and spring round ups of these huge herds would swell the payroll to double or even triple that number as white, Indian, black and Hispanic cowboys found work in bulldogging and branding. The yearly round up must have been a colorful sight in every sense of the word.

These ranches poured thousands of dollars each year into the local economy. But after the allotments, as land went from tribal to individual ownership, the large herds grazing on huge tracts of land virtually disappeared and the era of the wealthy cattle baron came to an end. Indian Territory -- soon to become the state of Oklahoma -- was no longer the pasturing ground for Texas cattle heading to market. But ranching continues today as one of the most profitable agricultural businesses in Oklahoma.

Agency Hill Site of Muskogee History

Muskogee had only been in existence a few years when the United States government decided to consolidate the agencies of the Five Tribes into one agency in July 1874. The first U.S. agent of the Consolidated Agency, as it was called then, had the task of deciding the location of the building to house his office. He persuaded the Creek Nation to convey to the government a section of land on a hill about three miles west of Muskogee. He called it Prospect Hill because this treeless height afforded a spectacular view of the surrounding prairie and looked down on the dusty cattle town of Muskogee sitting on the Texas Road and the Katy Railroad.

By the time the Agency building was completed in 1875, it was being called the Union Agency and the hill had been dubbed Agency Hill. Members of the Five Tribes would come to the Agency to conduct their business with the government. An 80-acre farm was a part of the Agency and the Indians would camp on the farm grounds while visiting the Agency. The Agency building itself could be seen for miles by travelers on the Texas Road or the Okmulgee Road.

After only a few years, the Agency office was moved into Muskogee to be closer to the roads and to local commerce. It was housed in the Turner Hardware Building next to the Katy Depot. The land on Agency Hill was reconveyed to the Creek Nation. The Creeks then leased the Agency building to the Baptist Home Mission Society to run a school for African American students. It was called Evangel Mission. The building has seen several other uses through the years. It is now the Five Civilized Tribes Museum.

In the early 1900s, Agency Hill was chosen as the site for a new water reservoir for the growing city of Muskogee. In 1903, Muskogee developed its first waterworks system and built a water reservoir on Standpipe Hill behind what is now Sadler Arts Academy. But water pressure was never very good because this reservoir didn't have enough height. So the city acquired part of Agency Hill and built a reservoir there to serve the increasing demand for water in town.

In November 1909, the Creek Nation conveyed an additional 40 acres of land to the city of Muskogee to be used as a city park. By this time the land the park was to occupy had become an overgrown bramble of trees and vines.

Another 55 acres of land in the area was purchased by Alice Robertson in 1910. She built her dream home here and called it Sawokla Farm. It was a working dairy and vegetable farm and she sold her produce at a small cafeteria in town that she called Sawokla Cafeteria. When she ran for Congress in 1920, Alice would hold big barbecues at the farm to raise funds for her campaign. The farmhouse burned in 1925.

While in Congress, Alice had worked to get a Veterans Hospital placed in Muskogee. Working with the other Oklahoma Congressional delegation, she developed a plan where the state would build the hospital and then lease it to the federal government. The Veterans Hospital opened in 1923 on land adjacent to Sawokla Farm on Agency Hill.

In the meantime, the city of Muskogee had been slowly developing the park on the hill. Following World War I, it was decided to name the park in honor of the veterans who had served in this "war to end all wars." The park was given the name Honor Heights Park in 1919. The park was more fully developed with WPA labor in the early 1930s.

Veterans again were honored on Agency Hill when the Rainbow Division Amphitheater was built and dedicated in 1976. The 42nd "Rainbow" Division had trained at Camp Gruber during World War II and these veterans remembered the hospitality they had received when visiting Muskogee. The amphitheater was built to face Camp Gruber and 300 Rainbow Division veterans attended its dedication.

Few locations in Muskogee have such historical significance as Agency Hill. Its importance is only matched by the beauty of the park built there.

Drought of 1874 Worst in Area History

Most of Indian Territory was devastated by the destruction and neglect that occurred during the Civil War. But this was not the most difficult time faced by the residents of the Three Rivers region. According to historian Grant Foreman, the summer of 1874 was the most "critical situation ever" in the territory with severe shortages of food bringing both people and animals to the point of starvation.

That summer had brought an extended drought to the region. Crops failed everywhere except for a few in the bottomlands closest to the rivers. And even here, the production was much less than what it normally would have been. Wells went dry and farmers and ranchers had to drive their stock for miles to the few springs or wells that did not fail.

As is often the case, the drought was made even worse because it was followed by a plague of grasshoppers. The sky would darken with the clouds of insects as they moved unstoppable across the dry land, stripping every bit of vegetation from the landscape. Augusta Robertson was teaching at Tullahassee Mission north of Muskogee that summer. She later recalled her students' fascination with the grasshoppers that settled in a solid mass on the fence around the mission turning the white pickets a muddy brown. The insects devoured the peach orchard, leaving empty peach stones hanging from leafless limbs.

Despite their destructiveness, though, both Augusta and her younger sister Grace recalled a strange beauty in the bugs. Their wings were iridescent in the sunlight as they took flight after eating everything in sight.

Nature added insult to injury by following the hot, dry summer with an especially cold winter. The poorer segments of the population were hardest hit by nature's cruelty. Many died from exposure and pneumonia. Others were driven to killing their livestock to eat and selling the hides to buy other food. They also foraged for roots and tree bark for nourishment, all that was left behind by the grasshoppers.

By the spring of 1875, tribal representatives were traveling to Washington to appeal for assistance to help feed their destitute population. The Creek Council tried to help its poorest members by authorizing merchants in Muskogee and other settlements in the Nation to extend credit of two dollars worth of food to over 1500 individuals. Many wealthy Cherokees opened their stores of food to help feed students at the schools. They allowed neighbors to water their stock at their wells and offered what other assistance they could.

Fortunately the severe weather did not last long. Pulling together, the people of the Three Rivers region survived the hard times and by 1876 were fully recovered and enjoying nature's bounty once again. At the dedication ceremony of the Union Agency, held in 1876, an outdoor barbecue feast was spread on the Agency grounds for the hundreds of people who attended the festivities. It was testimony to the strength and resilience of the people of Indian Territory.

Standing Rock Was Surrounded by Myths and Legends

One of the most curious and notable landmarks in the Three Rivers region was the Standing Rock located in the center of the Canadian River near Eufaula. This enormous sandstone rock rose out of the center of the riverbed which is the boundary between the Cherokee and Choctaw Nations. For centuries it was used as a way marker for Native Americans, explorers, immigrants and surveyors in Indian Territory. The Standing Rock became one of the cornerstone markers of the surveyed boundary line of the Cherokee Nation.

How this huge boulder came to stand in the middle of the river is a matter of conjecture for its existence predates any written history. It was noted in the journals of early explorers who plied the waters of the Canadian River. The most plausible explanation is that at one time it was actually a part of the bank of the river. A flood may have changed the river's channel and the rushing waters carved away the softer soil of the bank, leaving the rock standing in the middle of the river's new channel.

Whatever its history, the Standing Rock developed an aura of mystery. Legends grew up around it and each story grew larger with the telling over the years.

The rock was at least 20 feet tall and its sides were worn smooth by the centuries of water passing over it. The smooth walls of the Standing Rock would have been impossible to climb and the water eddied and swirled around the base of the rock making it difficult to reach by boat.

Yet old-timers said that a direction marker shaped like a hatchet had been carved at the top of the rock with its handle pointing toward the rugged hills of the Cherokee Nation's Canadian District.

According to a story printed in an 1899 edition of *Twin Territories* magazine, the mystery of the carved hatchet had to do with buried treasure. The story goes that a rancher had driven a herd of cattle to market in Kansas. On his return trip home, well-paid in silver coin for his cattle, he feared he was about to be robbed.

He left the main road and pushed back into the wilderness near Standing Rock in what was "Belle Starr" territory. Here he buried the silver, marking its position with carved directions. He returned to the main road and continued on south, expecting to return shortly and retrieve his treasure.

However when he reached Texas he fell ill. While under a doctor's care, the rancher realized he was dying and with his last words he whispered directions to the doctor, telling him how to find his buried coin. He was to look for the carved hatchet on the Standing Rock, follow the direction the handle pointed into the hills, find a carved arrow pointing toward a cave and dig for the treasure inside the cave.

At first the doctor dismissed the dying man's words. But later the idea of finding buried treasure intrigued him and he decided a vacation trip up to "the Indian Nations" wouldn't hurt. Finding the Standing Rock proved easy enough since it was such a well-known landmark. But the doctor found the area to be so rugged and remote and so full of "wild Indians" that he did not linger long. He returned to Texas without the treasure.

The doctor did, however, write to a Cherokee man in Indian Territory whom he knew only by reputation. He told him the story of the buried coin. This man supposedly went exploring and found the carved hatchet, the carved arrow, the cave and a hole dug in the cave floor – but no treasure. If it ever really existed, some other treasure hunter had already found it. This account was told to the *Twin Territories* editor by an old-timer named I.B. Hitchcock who claimed to have seen the letter written by the Texas doctor.

Whether this treasure actually existed seems unlikely, but we'll never know. The Standing Rock is now buried under the waters of Lake Eufaula. In times of drought the tip of the Standing Rock can be seen peeking out from the waters of the lake.

The Cattle Industry Was a Builder of Indian Territory

The era of the cattle drive is one of the most romanticized times in American history. The professional cowboy came into being at that time. It was following the Civil War and there was an enormous demand for beef, which had been in short supply during the war. Suddenly anyone in the cattle business could make money if they could just get their beef to market.

Texas was the largest cattle supplier, but many enterprising businessmen in Indian Territory began building their herds to take advantage of this lucrative opportunity. Cattle made the fortune for many Three Rivers area landowners.

Much of Indian Territory was still unfenced in the Cattle Trail Era of the 1870s and huge herds of longhorn cattle came up the trails to railheads like Muskogee. Many communities along the Katy railroad had a stockyard and Muskogee's was at the north end of town – about where the Arrowhead Mall is now located. The bellowing of the penned cattle waiting for transport on rail cars could be heard all over town.

Area ranchers also brought their cattle to market after letting them fatten on the open range across the Indian Nations. The Muscogee and Seminole Live Stock Association would meet in Muskogee to plan the annual roundup. Members of this association would cooperate in this massive roundup, thus enabling both large and small ranches to efficiently collect their scattered cattle.

The plan of the Live Stock Association was to divide the Muscogee and Seminole Nations as well as part of the Cherokee Nation into eleven sections. The first section consisted of the Canadian District of the Cherokee Nation and some of what today is Muskogee County. Cattle in this section were brought to the ranch of P.N. Blackstone and he would oversee the operation. The second district's roundup was to take place at the Three-Bar Ranch and ranchers Gentry, Lipscomb and Severs were in charge.

Also in the Three Rivers area was district five that included the Severs ranch near Muskogee and ranches as far west as Concharty Mountain. Cattle rounded up in this district were brought to the Severs ranch and Captain F.B. Severs led this operation.

After the meeting of the Live Stock Association, the individual ranchers returned home to begin preparations for the roundup. This might include hiring additional "cow hands" as well as getting equipment and holding pens prepared and buying provisions for the days spent out on the range.

During the roundup the cowboys from each ranch would fan out through their district, locate the grazing cattle and then drive them back to the selected rendezvous point. Then on a designated day, the ranchers would come to that site and separate out the cattle bearing their brand.

Each district had its own meeting date for separating the cattle and these dates were set at two-day intervals so every rancher could go to each rendezvous point and collect his livestock. In this way, a vast stretch of open land could be covered in a relatively short time and the cattle were quickly on their way to market.

Cooperative efforts like this were the hallmark of the early pioneers working to wrest a living from the frontier. From barn-raisings and quilting bees to threshing crews and cattle roundups, our forefathers and mothers knew the value of cooperation. Even competitors knew that if they worked together, everyone would benefit.

Calm Clerk Parried Knife Attack

In the early days of Indian Territory, smuggling liquor in from the surrounding states was an occupation followed by many unscrupulous characters. In fact, it may have been in Indian Territory that the term bootlegger was born. Smugglers would fit narrow flasks of whiskey into their high boots to slip them into the Territory and sell them in backwoods saloons or in the back rooms of legitimate businesses. The liquor sold by these whiskey peddlers was usually a strong, homemade brew that often proved the trigger for episodes of violence in area towns.

With law enforcement being somewhat limited in those days, residents of the Territorial towns had learned to quickly shutter their windows and blow out their kerosene lamps when gunshots were heard at night. Someone with too much to drink was out on a rampage and they would shoot at anything that moved.

Even in broad daylight, incidents of violence brought on by liquor were not unheard of. The intention wasn't always robbery or revenge, but sometimes just sheer meanness by men who had spent too much time with the bottle. Sometimes a touch of grim comedy was mingled with these tragic events.

One such event occurred in Muskogee in the late 1870s when a young man rode into town after a night of revelry had left him very drunk. Brandishing a bowie knife, this young desperado entered a number of downtown stores, driving the clerks out before him with his threats of violence.

Rushing into Patterson's Mercantile at the corner of Main and Broadway, he sent the clerks flying outside for dear life. He reached Andrew Robb at the counter and slashed the brim from his straw hat with his bowie knife. Fortunately, the young man rushed on without stopping to discover that the strike had only reached the hat and not Mr. Robb's head.

At the stairway of the store, he met T.F. Meagher who had just come downstairs, carrying an armload of merchandise. Meagher was trapped with his back to the closed door leading upstairs and had no other way of escape. Keeping his wits about him, Mr. Meagher extended his hand to the drunken desperado, never dropping the supplies he carried.

"Why, good afternoon, sir," Meagher said with absolute coolness. "I hope you are well. Are the folks at home all well? What can I show you this afternoon? I suppose you want to do a little trading."

Met with such calm reasonableness, the drunken man sheathed his bowie knife and shook hands with Mr. Meagher, suddenly remembering that there was some trading he needed to do. And so for the moment peace was restored in Muskogee.

Federal Court in Fort Smith Brought Justice to Indian Territory

For the first half of the 19th century laws and courts in Indian Territory were confusing and often ineffective. Each of the Five Civilized Tribes had a judicial system with jurisdiction over their own tribal members. The tribes, however, had little recourse in dealing with non-Indians and the criminal element from surrounding states frequently exploited this situation.

In 1851 the U.S. District Court in Arkansas was divided into two districts and the western district was given jurisdiction over "the Indian country." The courthouse was located at Van Buren. But for years this court proved weak, corrupt and generally incapable of dealing with the growing crime problem foisted upon the citizens of Indian Territory.

Following the Civil War, the Van Buren court was moved to Fort Smith. It occupied a two-story brick building next to the "Hole in the Wall" Saloon. Court was held on the second floor; prisoners were kept in the basement.

It wasn't until the appointment of Judge Isaac Parker in 1875 that the Fort Smith court began to have any impact on crime in Indian Territory. Parker came to the court from Missouri and proved to be tireless in his pursuit of justice. During his 21 years on the bench, Parker presided over 13,000 court cases with over 9,000 convictions, 160 death sentences and 79 hangings. His court was in session 6 days of the week and closed only for Sundays and Christmas.

Some of the most notorious criminals of Indian Territory passed through Parker's courtroom – Cherokee Bill, Ned Christie, Sam and Belle Starr, and several members of the Dalton Gang. They all were subjected to Parker's fierce rhetoric in condemning their criminal activity. Parker often ended his fiery speeches with the words, "May God whose laws you have broken and before whose tribunal you must appear, have mercy on your soul."

Mercy was not liberally handed out in Judge Parker's courtroom. He had increased the marshal's corps when he came to the court and this small army of lawmen scoured Indian Territory serving warrants at $2 per arrest. The persistent pursuit of justice under Isaac Parker had a positive effect. Slowly criminal activity was brought in check.

In 1889, a federal court was established in Muskogee. The Fort Smith court continued to try serious felony crimes, but a flood of civil and misdemeanor cases came to the Muskogee court. Judge James Shackleford quickly replaced Judge Parker as the busiest judge in the Southwest.

Party Loyalty Among Creeks Sometimes Led to War

From the time of their removal from the southeastern United States to Indian Territory, members of the Creek Nation had been bitterly divided over many issues. As with other tribes who were moved to Indian Territory, some Creeks had favored emigration while others had opposed it vigorously. Once settled in Indian Territory, the conflict among Creek factions continued into the Civil

War with the loyalties of tribal members split between the Union and the Confederacy.

The Creek Nation wrote a new constitution following the Civil War and worked to rebuild after the devastation of that conflict. But factions still existed within the tribe and elections for principal chief were often bitterly fought contests.

Three loosely organized political parties functioned in the 1880s. They were the Muscogee party led by James Perryman, the Loyal party led by Isparhecher and the Pin party led by Sam Checote. Party differences often led to armed resistance from those not in power in the Creek government.

In 1882, Isparhecher was serving as a judge of the Okmulgee District and Sam Checote was principal chief. The Pin party made up most of the Creek legislature as well. Accused of "sedition" by the legislature, Isparhecher was impeached and removed from office. Embarrassed and outraged, Isparhecher gathered about 350 Loyal followers and set up a camp near Nuyaka. He established a quasi government, declared himself chief, and established a lighthorse military division, issuing arms and munitions.

Pleasant Porter, who had been representing the Creek Nation in Washington, was called home to help quell this disturbance. Porter had military experience and had served as commander of the Creek Lighthorsemen at one time.

Porter gathered a force of 700 men and succeeded in driving Isparhecher's men out of the Creek Nation westward into the Sac and Fox Nation. While little actual fighting took place during this event, it was referred to as the Green Peach War because it took place while the peaches were still green in the orchards of the Creek Nation.

Having no authority to pursue Isparhecher's men outside the Creek Nation, Porter turned the matter over to the U.S. military. Four units of the Ninth Cavalry, an African-American division, were dispatched from Forts Sill and Reno and Isparhecher's men were captured and taken to Fort Gibson.

General Clinton Fisk, who ran for President in 1884, was chairing the Board of Indian Commissioners at this time. He came to Muskogee to negotiate a peace treaty between the Isparhecher and Checote parties. Arriving late in the week, he issued a summons to all concerned parties to be present on Monday morning for a conference to iron out differences among the tribe.

On Monday, everyone was present but Sam Checote. To General Fisk's annoyance, the chief did not arrive until Tuesday morning. He explained that he did not receive the summons to the conference until late Saturday evening. Being a Christian and an ordained Methodist minister, he chose not to break the Sabbath by traveling on Sunday. Therefore he could not get to Muskogee until Tuesday. General Fisk "thanked him and stated he would be careful never again to call a meeting that would require travel on Sunday."

It took a week for all of the parties to express their grievances and come to an agreement for ending the conflict. A treaty was signed and a service to commemorate the event was held at the Rock Church in Muskogee. Thus the Green Peach War quietly came to an end.

Photographers Chronicled Early River Life

While the invention of photography dates to the early 1800s, it is safe to say that few, if any, cameras were in Indian Territory before the Civil War. Life among the Native Americans on the frontier was chronicled by artists such as George Catlin. Early visitors sometimes made sketches of their visits for mapping and scientific study.

But photographs would not record Indian Territory until after the railroad began to bring many new people into the region.

One of the first photographers in Muskogee was a man named J.F. Standiford. A West Virginian by birth, Standiford arrived here in 1878 after working in Illinois and Kansas. He paid the permit required by the Creek Nation to operate a business here and built his home and photography studio. For many years he was advertised as the only "licensed" photographer in Indian Territory.

In those days, photographers were like traveling salesmen. They did not wait for customers to come to their studio to have their portrait made. Carrying their cumbersome equipment with them, these photographers traveled by wagon from farm to farm offering to photograph the family residing there. This was the primary way in which they made their living as photographers.

Standiford enjoyed travel so he covered most of Indian Territory in looking for work. He was a prolific artist and many of his photographs survive to this day. A Standiford photograph is often printed on very thick card stock with a decorative border framing the picture. Often Standiford would identify his photos as having been taken in "The Beautiful Indian Territory."

Standiford's wife and sister assisted him in his photography business, handling the chore of developing the negatives. The photographer had invented a revolving printing mechanism for his darkroom, said to be one of a kind. He also invented an "electric retouching apparatus" for which he took out a patent.

Other photography studios were established in Muskogee in later years. Alice Robertson ran a studio and is credited with many photographs taken in Muskogee around the time of statehood. An African American photographer named William Greene also had a studio on Second Street in Muskogee. He was best known for his portraits and some stunning examples of his work still survive today.

Without the work of these early day photographers, our understanding of the past would be greatly diminished. The record of the life of our ancestors creates a connection to the past that continues to fascinate us today.

6

Twin Territories

Ghost Stories Surround the Death of Belle Starr

In February of 1889, Belle Starr was shot and killed as she rode toward her home at Younger's Bend on the Canadian River. That same year a story began circulating about folks in the area seeing a ghost in the exact likeness of the Bandit Queen. The ghost reportedly would wander through the hills around Younger's Bend on moonlit nights.

The story grew over the years, as stories like this often do, growing larger with each telling. It got to the point that locals around the Whitefield area were hesitant to go hunting for possum across the Canadian River when there was a full moon out.

According to Stoney Hardcastle a historian and teacher, the ghostly legend says Belle would "ride off that mountain where she's buried and ride down toward the river at Younger's Bend." Supposedly, she had gold buried there and "she is going to get you if you were looking for her gold."

Or another version that has been told around campfires for over a hundred years is that when the moon is full, Belle's ghost comes riding down from the mountain on the north side of the river and gallops on the wind down into the river valley. And you can hear her singing. Belle loved to play the piano and sing.

Perhaps the horse is Venus, said to be Belle's favorite; its likeness was carved on her tombstone. This horse was shot and killed when a posse was chasing her husband Sam through a cornfield so, of course, the horse is a ghost too. Other stories say she rides from the site of her grave in Younger's Bend and heads southward looking for her gold hidden in a hollow tree.

Another belief about Belle's ghost is that she is not searching for lost gold but rather is seeking revenge for her unsolved murder. According to this story, her ghost would be coming from the spot on the south side of the river known as Hoyt Bottom where she was shot off her horse and killed. If so, her ghost would be hunting for her killer.

There were a number of suspects at the time of her death including her neighbor Edgar Watson and her last husband Jim July. Watson was tried for the murder, but not convicted. No one else was ever arrested or tried. And the number of suspects has grown through the years to include even her son.

Others believe there is nothing sinister in these legendary ghostly appearances. Belle is said to have had a flair for the dramatic so perhaps she aspired to the stage during her lifetime. It may be that on moonlit nights when Belle rides through the Canadian River valley, she is simply showing off. Either way, no one wants to be caught out at midnight when the wind moans through the river valley and the moon is full.

Skeletons Found in Old Graveyard

When Matthew Arbuckle and the Seventh Infantry built Fort Gibson on the bank of the Grand River in 1824, it seemed like the ideal location for an army outpost. Accessible by navigable rivers and the already well-worn Texas Road, the fort could easily be kept supplied and manned. In fact, Fort Gibson, as the Army's westernmost post, was often the billet for more troops than all the other frontier forts combined.

But this "ideal location" soon proved deadly. Because the rivers flooded each fall and spring, the fort was frequently under water and mosquitoes and disease were rampant.

With its crowded conditions, the fort's hospital was often swamped with soldiers suffering from fever and dysentery. Serving at Fort Gibson truly proved to be "hazardous duty," for more soldiers died from disease than from any other cause. Fort Gibson was called in Army circles, "the graveyard of the west."

The actual graveyard for the fort filled rapidly with soldiers and civilians who were hastily buried, wrapped in the blanket from their bed to prevent any further spread of disease. The site for the cemetery was also poorly chosen for it was on a piece of ground west of the fort that sloped down toward the river.

When the Fort Gibson National Cemetery was established in 1868, many of the soldiers buried in the fort graveyard were moved to the new cemetery. However, by that time, many graves were no longer marked so the remains of both soldiers and civilians were left in the old graveyard.

Over time, rain and floods had washed many grave markers into the river and the soil began to wear away from the slope creating deep gullies through the old cemetery surrounded by a low stone wall. The graveyard fell into neglect and was soon grown over with brush and weeds. Many forgot that it even existed.

The *Fort Gibson Post* newspaper reported in 1898 that F.J. Boudinot was out walking through the area of the old cemetery one day when he happened upon a gruesome sight. Stepping off into one of the gullies, he found the gleaming white bones of a skeleton, exposed by soil erosion. The blue cloth of a soldier's uniform was badly deteriorated, but the gold buttons and insignia remained. A rusted sword lay nearby, apparently buried with its owner.

Boudinot took the skeleton and sword of this unknown soldier to a local doctor who displayed them in his office, creating shivers of dark fascination among all who came to view them. The newspaper sent a reporter out to the old graveyard and he too discovered several skeletons, glistening in the sunlight and exposed to the ravages of time and the elements.

The *Post* stated that some folks who lived in the "Old Town," as the early section of Fort Gibson was called, claimed "that when the north wind howls dismally and the nights are dark and moonless, weird-looking lights may be seen flitting to and fro and strange noises [can be] heard in the vicinity." Stories of "haunts" soon circulated among the more superstitious folks and no one wanted to be caught out near the old graveyard at night.

Scarcity of Schools Created Demand for Education

Education in Indian Territory's early days was a patchwork system set up by the various tribes and by different mission organizations and churches. From the beginning, schools were generally segregated, often even separating boys and girls.

Schools for Native American students were first established by the missions of the Presbyterian, Methodist and Baptist congregations. Some, such as the Union Mission near Mazie, operated as early as the 1820s. The

Union Mission offered school first to the Osage and then to Cherokee and Creek students.

By the 1830s, as the removals were completed, all of the Five Tribes had established schools for their own tribal members. Mission schools continued to be established throughout the Three Rivers region at places like Tullahassee, Park Hill, Tulasi, Koweta, and Nuyaka.

Following the Civil War, some of these mission schools began to teach the children of freedmen. Tullahassee Mission became one such school for Creek freedmen. The Union Agency building, which now houses the Five Civilized Tribes Museum, was used as Evangel Mission, a boarding school for African American children.

Schools for non-tribal children were scarce at first. As towns began to develop along the rail lines in the 1870s, and more and more white and black settlers moved into Indian Territory, the need for schools for their children became acute.

In towns such as Muskogee, subscription schools were started for both black and white students. Parents could pay a "subscription" or tuition for their children to attend. The tuition averaged around $1.50 per child. In rural areas, education was often neglected altogether. Children were either schooled at home, walked for miles to the nearest subscription school, or received no education at all.

In 1898, with the passage of the Curtis Act, towns in Indian Territory could finally incorporate, elect a city government, raise taxes and establish public services such as water, sewer, streets and schools. Muskogee residents elected their first school board in July 1898.

The school board rented and renovated a building located on South Second Street between Okmulgee Ave. and Boston. It had originally been a Presbyterian school and then had housed Alice Robertson's Minerva Home for Girls and later Henry Kendall College.

This was to be a graded school for white students. A principal and four teachers were hired. So many students wanted to attend the school, the board had to offer a morning school and an afternoon school. Even then some students had to be turned away.

A suitable rent facility could not be found for black students so the school board spent $2,000 erecting a new frame building at the corner of Sixth and Market Streets. Four teachers were hired for this school as well, and it too was quickly swamped with students wanting a free public education. Immediate plans were made and sites were chosen to establish more schools in each of the city's wards.

In 1955, Oklahoma's new governor, Raymond Gary, proposed an amendment to the Oklahoma constitution in response to the Supreme Court decision of *Brown vs. Topeka Board of Education*. The amendment would change the way schools were funded in Oklahoma, thus opening the door for desegregation. Oklahomans supported the amendment as State Question 368, called the "Better Schools Amendment," in April 1955. Desegregation of schools in the region began quickly in some communities and continued until the early 1970s.

Creek Poet Authored State Constitution

Alexander Posey was a leader in the Creek Nation and is considered to be one of the greatest Native American poets. He wrote his poetry under the pen name Chinnubbie Harjo and many newspapers carried his writings. He was born near Eufaula in 1873 just after that town developed along the Katy Railroad. He grew up on a farm and attended Bacone College (then called Indian University) in Muskogee.

Posey served as superintendent of the Creek Orphan School at Wealaka and the Eufaula Creek High School. He also was Superintendent of Public Instruction for the entire Creek Nation. For a time, he edited the *Indian Journal* newspaper published in Eufaula.

His letters to the editor from a fictional character named Fus Fixico were reprinted by papers around the world. He wrote in a popular style of the day called "dialect writing" in which he recreated the Creek-English that he heard among the full-blood members of the tribe. Through Fus Fixico, Posey satirized the current political situation in ways that were humorous but pointedly critical of how the tribes were being treated.

Alexander Posey was the individual who wrote about the name and origin for the Muscogee people. In 1902 the new town was founded west of Eufaula. The town's name was Spokogee and according to Mr. Posey, this was the original name of his people, predating the name Muscogee. He stated that the meaning of this word is "true blood."

In 1905 Posey was a delegate to the Sequoyah State Convention held at the Hinton Theater in Muskogee. He was elected secretary of the Convention and served on the Constitution Committee. Because he was a gifted writer, Posey was selected to write the Sequoyah Constitution and he produced a 35,000-word document that later served as the model for the Oklahoma Constitution.

In 1908, Posey met a tragic end when he drowned in the rain-swollen Canadian River. He was buried in Greenhill Cemetery in Muskogee. His wife later published a collection of his poems and still later the Fus Fixico letters were compiled into a book. His beautiful poetry and his life's work in education reflected his pride in his Native American heritage and desire to pass the thoughts of his fellow Creeks to future generations.

Cotton Was once King in Three Rivers Region

When the Five Civilized Tribes were removed from their homelands in the southeastern states to Indian Territory, they brought with them their Southern way of life. Many had owned large plantations and kept slaves for the production of cotton, which was very labor-intensive. They brought this practice to the Three Rivers area and the rich river bottomland soon was settled with cotton plantations.

Cotton production grew in the area until it was devastated by the conflict of the Civil War. Most of the Native Americans in Indian Territory fled either to Kansas or Texas, depending upon their loyalties. Only subsistence farming took place during the war.

Following the emancipation of slaves, many of the freedmen slipped away from their former masters who had taken them to Texas and they returned to the homes they had known on the river plantations. These freedmen settled into cotton production as did many white tenant farmers who moved into the Territory when the railroads arrived. Cotton was a major crop in the region for many years.

Cotton was not a wildly profitable crop because it required so much hand labor. By the time the landowner had paid his laborers and his creditors – for he always had to borrow against the crop – he rarely did more than break even. But cotton production employed hundreds of workers and it propped up the local economy with those jobs.

Besides the planting and harvesting of cotton, gins and mills to process the cotton and cottonseed were also major employers in the area. Almost every community in the region had at least one cotton gin located somewhere near the railroad tracks that passed through the town.

Some towns had several gins and Muskogee was no exception. In 1899, the Patterson Cotton Gin, one of Muskogee's largest, handled 4,380 bales of cotton, bought from farmers who came from all over the region. It paid out over $65,000 to cotton farmers for their product that same year. During the harvest season, the cotton gins would run night and day compressing the fleecy product into bales to be shipped out on the railroad to markets all over the world.

The gins extracted the cottonseed from the bolls and this by-product provided employment in a secondary industry. The Muskogee Cotton Oil Mill Company was a leading industry in Muskogee around the turn of the last century. Employing over 60 men, this mill paid out $100 thousand for cottonseed in 1899 and had a capacity of 60 tons of crushed seeds per day. The oil was shipped out in tankers and the crushed seed was sold to local stockyards for cattle feed.

But cotton did not remain king in the Three Rivers region. When the price of cotton plummeted in the 1930s, it simply was no longer profitable. Farmers either abandoned their land and moved away or switched to the production of more profitable crops such as wheat, corn or soybeans. Much of the land was returned to the native prairie and used as range for cattle. Today, cotton production in Oklahoma is limited to only the southwestern counties.

The Rivers Weren't Muskogee's First Water Supply

In its earliest years, Muskogee had a problem with water supply – ironic for a town sitting at the confluence of three rivers. Muskogee had developed quickly on the railroad line with nothing in the way of townsite planning. True streets were an unheard of luxury in early-day Muskogee and a water system was a dream for the dim and distant future.

Despite occasional droughts, water was abundant in the Three Rivers area. Accessing the water was the problem. An old cistern was located where the road to Okmulgee crossed Main Street in Muskogee. Whether it tapped ground water or simply caught rainwater is unclear, but its location is marked on early maps.

The well probably predated the city and may have been used by an early farmer in the area. It was considered the community water source when the town was just getting started and it was adequate to serve the few first families who settled in Muskogee. But the town's growth quickly outpaced this water supply.

Many residents dug their own wells or cisterns, or kept rain barrels to catch the soft water for their households. A few early entrepreneurs went into the business of supplying water for the growing town. Otto Zufall was a mulewhacker (a freight hauler who used a mule team and wagon) by trade, but he hauled water as well. He charged 75 cents for a barrel of drinking water possibly from the Katy Pond and 50 cents for household water from a nearby creek. Possibly it was Coodey's Creek south of town.

Charles Willey, called "Uncle Charlie" by most everyone in town, began hauling water also for a small per-barrel fee. He discovered a spring of water out in the country at what later became the intersection of Eighth and Broadway. He dug out a well to collect the water and built a small springhouse over it. Then with a pair of small donkeys, he would load up a wagon with five barrels of water and deliver it to residents and businesses in town.

Springs of water were quite numerous in the Muskogee area and were often the cleanest source of water available. Captain Severs built his hotel on State Street over a spring and the cistern for it can still be seen in the lowest section of the Severs Building basement. And the Union Agency was plagued with flooding in its basement because it had been built over a spring as well.

The first effort at piping water in Muskogee was put together by a group of downtown businessmen. They connected to the Katy water tank near the pond which sat where Arrowhead Mall is now located. The water pipe ran under Main Street from Fondulac (now Martin Luther King Street) to Okmulgee Avenue with valves set at intervals where the businesses along the street could tap into it. Over time however, the Katy Pond became a polluted dumping point and its water was no longer usable. Once again the town had surpassed its water supply.

After Muskogee formed its municipal government in 1898, it would seem logical to make a water system its first priority. But schools and paved streets took precedent and it wasn't until 1903 that the city began its waterworks program. Laying pipe from Three Forks, Muskogee first took its water from the Arkansas River and later from the cleaner Grand River. That river, through the Fort Gibson reservoir, still provides drinking water today, not only for Muskogee but for many surrounding communities that now connect to Muskogee's water supply.

Moores Key Couple for Creeks, Haskell

In November of 1882, Augusta Robertson, a teacher and daughter of missionaries William and Ann Eliza Robertson, married Napoleon Bonaparte Moore who was a leader in Creek politics. He owned a 200-acre ranch called Mule Shoe Ranch located near present-day Haskell. Their home was a large log cabin and it was for many years a social center for the area bringing many influential Indian leaders to the Choska Bottoms to meet with Judge Moore.

N.B. Moore had served in various capacities in Creek government including four years in the House of Warriors and another four in the House of Kings at Okmulgee, the nation's capital. At the time of his marriage to Augusta, he was serving as a supreme court judge for the Creek Nation. He worked with Joshua Ross in Muskogee to develop the International Indian Fair that was first held in the early 1870s at what today is Spaulding Park.

In 1888, Judge Moore was appointed treasurer for the Creek Nation and he conducted much of the business of the tribe at Mule Shoe Ranch. Augusta resigned from her position at Nuyaka Mission School and was a great help to her husband in managing the financial affairs of the tribe. She was given the nickname, "the Little Treasurer," because she handled the day-to-day work of keeping the books and paying the bills for the Creek Nation.

In 1889, the Moores traveled to Washington, D.C. to meet with government leaders about financial assistance to the tribe. One meeting was with President Benjamin Harrison and Augusta later wrote that the President treated them with great disdain. They were able to get the financial aid package passed through Congress, however.

The Moores were involved in the community of Haskell after it developed. In 1908 the Moores contributed to the construction of Haskell's third church. Named the Robertson Memorial Presbyterian Church, it was built with a generous donation from Augusta and her husband to honor her father William Robertson, the great missionary who had labored so faithfully for years at Tullahassee Mission.

The church was built of native stones on West Commercial Street. It was dedicated in a service on April 18, 1909 with Dr. Grant Evans, president of Henry Kendall College (later Tulsa University) as the guest speaker. This church still stands today as one of Haskell's truly historic buildings.

The Moores continued to live at Mule Shoe Ranch for the remainder of their lives and were active in community affairs. Augusta helped to start the Red Cross in Haskell just as her sister Alice had in Muskogee. Both

Augusta and N.B. Moore were buried in the Haskell Cemetery.

Citizens Took Stand Against Crime

For several months during 1894, the Cook Gang terrorized much of Indian Territory. Members of the group, led by Bill Cook, were from around the Fort Gibson area, but their crime spree took them through the Cherokee and Creek Nations.

They robbed a bank in Chandler, a store in Okmulgee, a train at Claremore and the Katy Station at Chouteau in addition to waylaying travelers around the Muskogee area. As their crimes continued, panic began to build in the area. The Indian Agent, D.M. Wisdom, wired Washington requesting assistance in capturing the lawless gang.

The U.S. Attorney General and the Cherokee Chief C.J. Harris issued warrants for the arrest of gang members. Federal marshals, with the help of the Texas Rangers, began to round up Cook Gang members and Bill Cook was brought to trial in Judge Isaac Parker's court in Fort Smith.

However, some Cook Gang members were still at large in April 1895. Sam McWilliams, also known as the Verdigris Kid, George Sanders and Sam Butler were still on the scout and were still boldly engaging in criminal acts.

Early one Thursday morning in April, the three rode into Braggs. Dismounting their horses at the local hotel, they immediately started shooting and ordered everyone in sight to raise their hands. Everyone complied, included deputy marshal Ed Barbee, whom the outlaws disarmed.

The gang members marched their prisoners to the Madden Mercantile where they shot a store clerk trying to escape. The Verdigris Kid and his cohorts proceeded to rob the store, including picking out new boots for each of them. Tom Madden, owner of the store was at his home only a short distance from the store. He heard the shot and could clearly see what was taking place at his business.

Grabbing his gun, he was about to confront the robbers, but his wife persuaded him to alert others in town and seek their assistance. This he did, rounding up two deputy sheriffs from their homes along with other townsmen. Taking position at a store nearby, they opened fire when the outlaws came out of the mercantile.

The Verdigris Kid was hit and went down. Marshal Barbee then picked up the fallen man's Winchester and began to fire as well. Both Sanders and Butler were shot also, but Butler was able to mount his horse and ride out of town. McWilliams and Sanders died of their wounds and their bodies were transported to Fort Smith.

This brought an end to the crimes spree and terror of the Cook Gang. But unfortunately it was not the end of outlaw gangs who continued to rob banks and trains even after statehood and the fight against such crime continued. The struggle to overcome crime sometimes meant ordinary citizens had to take an extraordinary stand for right.

Three Rivers Region Experienced Oil Boom Early

The first oil well in the US is considered to be the Drake Well drilled in Pennsylvania in 1859. This was the first time a well was sunk for the express purpose of extracting oil for commercial use. It opened up the petroleum industry and eventually changed the world economy.

Native Americans had used the natural "seeps" of oil for generations, but it was primarily considered to have medicinal uses until Edwin Drake drilled his well in Pennsylvania. In Indian Territory, members of the Five

Civilized Tribes were aware of oil's existence in their nations, but without efficient ways to extract it, or a demand for it, there was little interest in drilling wells.

There are differing accounts about where the first oil well was drilled in Indian Territory. One source says that Lewis Ross was digging a salt well on the Grand Saline of the Grand River in 1859 and hit oil instead. His well produced about 10 gallons of oil a day for about a year. Another source says a well near Wapanucka in Atoka County was the first, dating to 1875. How much it produced is unclear. Still another source states that the first "deep" well was drilled in 1884 near Lehigh.

In 1897, a well was drilled near Bartlesville that seems to have been the trigger to attract investors to the territory in search of oil. In Muskogee, investors had already incorporated the Creek Oil and Gas Company as early as September 1895. A number of Muskogee's leading citizens were involved in this company. They drilled a well near the Severs Cotton Gin east of the Katy tracks in October of 1896, and struck oil at twelve hundred feet. Production was limited, however, because they did not have the facilities to store or ship the oil.

By the early 1900s oil and gas production was spreading across the Three Rivers area as more investors put money into oil exploration and drilling. Another well was drilled in Muskogee in 1903 and this set off a frenzy of drilling. Soon a "forest" of oil derricks was cropping up south of Muskogee. This brought the attention of refiners and Oklahoma's first oil refinery was established here. The Muskogee Oil Refinery produced kerosene, lubricating oil and industrial fuel, beginning in 1905.

Oil production in the Muskogee area continued into the 1930s but larger strikes in other locations eventually brought an end to the oil boom there. However, it continued in many other areas of Oklahoma. There are a number of Oklahoma oil wells on the National Register of

Historic Places including the Old Faucet Well in Atoka County, the Nellie Johnstone No. 1 at Bartlesville and the Nancy Taylor No. 1, near Haskell, drilled in 1916 by oilman J. Paul Getty.

Enforcing Temperance Was a Constant Crusade

From the earliest days of Indian Territory, it had been the policy of the federal government to keep the Indian country free of alcohol. It was a common belief of the day that the consumption of alcohol stirred the Indian to the warpath and it was also used by unscrupulous traders to take advantage of the native people. Concerned about the negative impact of liquor, most leaders -- both among the government and the tribes -- wanted Indian Territory to remain "dry."

Keeping it dry was the challenge. Early Native American ministers organized temperance societies among the tribes. The members of these societies pledged to abstain from alcohol and to fight its consumption among their communities. That didn't keep traders such as A.P. Chouteau and Sam Houston from shipping barrels of whiskey into the Three Forks area, however. This brought complaints to the government by missionaries at Union, Dwight and Fairfield Missions against Houston whom some Cherokees called "the Big Drunk."

Lawmen such as Samuel Sixkiller built their reputations on fighting bootleggers and whiskey runners. Sixkiller recognized that the unregulated flow of whiskey was behind much of the lawlessness of the Territory and he became relentless in tracking down the illegal caches of alcohol. One story is told about Captain Sixkiller finding bottles of the homemade brew stashed within the hollowed out logs of a bootlegger's cabin.

Women took up the fight against alcohol too. Mrs. Laura Harsha helped organize the Women's Christian Temperance Union in Muskogee in 1884. The story is told that Mrs. Harsha would visit the different stores in town to see if anything stronger than beer was being sold. If she found something suspicious, she would demand a sample which she would then take to a chemist for analysis. If her suspicions proved correct, she would turn the offending merchant in to the authorities.

Another marshal who fought against homemade stills was James "Bud" Ledbetter. He was known to haul in stashes from the hills and hollows around the region and then smash the bottles against the brick wall of the federal courthouse. When the famous (some would say infamous) temperance leader Carrie Nation visited Muskogee in 1906, she presented Ledbetter with a "golden hatchet" lapel pin. Nation had built her notoriety by taking a hatchet to saloons in the Kansas and Oklahoma area.

All these efforts, however, only slowed the flow of alcohol, but never completely stopped it. The proponents of the National Prohibition of Alcohol which culminated in the Eighteenth Amendment might only have looked to Indian Territory to know how their efforts would turn out.

Boys of Summer Took to the Fields of Indian Territory

Like everywhere else in America, baseball has been a popular sport in Oklahoma for well over a century. It was a "portable" game, requiring only a couple of bats, a few balls, some gloves and a handful of players on each team. It could be played on any makeshift field around any town on any occasion and often was. Sacks of hay or tin cans might mark the bases on prairie baseball diamonds in empty lots or at the outskirts of town.

Soldiers at Fort Gibson may have played the first baseball games in Indian Territory, bringing it with them from back east. The Cherokee Male Seminary in Tahlequah boasted of a winning baseball team as early as 1885. Bacone Indian University and Henry Kendall College in Muskogee also had early teams. And it wasn't uncommon for businesses to field a team among their employees as a way of advertising their business. Both the Patterson Mercantile and the Harsha & Spaulding Mercantile were known to have baseball teams around 1900.

By 1889, Joe "Iron Man" McGinnity, who later played in the major leagues, was organizing town teams in Indian Territory. Checotah, Tahlequah, Eufaula and Wagoner all had teams in the 1890s. Muskogee had both white and black teams for a number of years.

Makeshift stands for fans of the game consisted of planks placed on empty barrels. Rules for fans were simple: No alcohol, no betting, no profane language and killing the umpire was strictly forbidden. On any Sunday during the summer a sandlot game was being played somewhere and only the fall harvest brought an end to this summer pleasure.

As baseball grew to a professional sport, minor league teams were developed in Oklahoma. Around WWI, 37 towns in Oklahoma had minor league teams including Muskogee and Okmulgee who were part of the Western Association. Muskogee's minor league baseball field, called Athletic Park, was located where the Civic Center is today.

In 1922, the New York Yankees, including their most famous player Babe Ruth, played an exhibition game against the Brooklyn Dodgers at Athletic Park. The Yankees, like many other ball teams visiting Muskogee, stayed at the Severs Hotel because it was close enough for the players to walk to Athletic Park.

Banking Started Slow, But Proved Strong in Oklahoma

For most of Indian Territory's existence, banks were unheard of in the small towns of the Five Civilized Tribes. One reason was that cash itself was often scarce and for many years residents of the Territory relied on the barter system or lived on credit until the crops came in. Payment for the crops was then turned over to the local mercantile to pay off the debt that had accumulated through the growing season.

Because the merchants were the men with the money, they often took on the role of banker in Indian Territories early towns. In Muskogee the Patterson Mercantile and Spaulding Mercantile began providing banking services to the cattlemen, farmers and other settlers in the area. At first they simply allowed people to store cash in their safes since lawlessness and theft was an early problem.

Then the merchants began to offer loans, accepted deposits and kept records of accounts, and even made payments for individuals on their own checks. Some merchants, such as Homer Spaulding, even issued their own currency. It was called scrip and locals referred to the paper notes as "Spaulding scrip." It was used primarily to purchase goods in the Spaulding store, but other people around town would accept it for payments as well.

There were no legal means to establish a bank in Indian Territory until 1890, but in that year towns such as Muskogee, Ardmore, McAlester and Tahlequah saw national banks established. This became possible because Congress had extended existing banking laws to Indian Territory that year.

But smaller towns found it difficult to meet the stringent requirements of the National Banking Act and few national banks were established outside of the primary cities. Banks in Oklahoma Territory were as scarce and as loosely managed as the Indian Territory banks.

A financial panic in 1893 caused many depositors to lose their funds, causing a distrust of banks in the Twin Territories. The difficulties of the 1893 Panic were still on the minds of bankers and politicians as the Twin Territories approached statehood. Then in October 1907 another banking panic occurred just before statehood. Everyone said something needed to be done to protect depositors' money.

Addressing this need was a high priority for Muskogeean Charles N. Haskell after he was sworn in as Oklahoma's first governor. Calling for laws that would protect depositors, Haskell helped push a general banking bill through the state legislature. It was called the Oklahoma Bank Guarantee Law and it would become a model for the nation. This law created a Bank Guaranty Fund which consisted of a levy of 1 percent of average daily deposits from state banks.

In the next few years, as banks failed or were closed, the Bank Guaranty Fund ensured that no depositor lost a dollar. Though not without its critics, the system was declared a success by Governor Haskell. The Bank Guaranty Fund only continued until 1923, but it would serve as a model for other states and eventually for similar federal legislation.

First Bank in Indian Territory Occupied the Severs Block in Muskogee

For years, Indian Territory functioned without banks or currency of any kind. None of the tribes issued currency so residents of the Territory often found coin to be scarce. Most farmers and laborers used credit at the area mercantiles, borrowing against future crops or bartering for goods with livestock, produce or handcrafted items.

By 1889, Muskogee was one of the leading towns in Indian Territory with the federal court located here. Local merchants recognized that in order for their businesses and town to continue to grow, a bank was needed. But organizing a bank proved difficult.

Efforts of leading citizens such as Robert Owen, the U.S. Agent to the Five Civilized Tribes, and merchants such as A.W. Robb and Frederick Severs to charter a bank were frustrated. The Attorney General of the United States issued the opinion that banking laws of the United States did not apply to Indian Territory.

Owen lobbied for an extension of the National Banking Act to Indian Territory and pressed for the bank's charter. On June 7, 1890, one was issued, establishing the First National Bank of Muscogee. With this charter, the first bank in Indian Territory came into being.

The board of directors for the new bank included some of the Territory's most prominent citizens – Owen, Robb, Severs, T.B. Needles, P.J. Byrne, Clarence Turner and Leo Bennett of Muskogee and C.E. Foley of Eufaula, and J.E. Reynolds of South McAlester. The bank opened for business on August 22, 1890 in a new building on prime real estate in Muskogee.

At the time, three men claimed most of the property in and around Muskogee – Frederick Severs and Pleasant Porter of the Creek Nation and Robert Owen of the Cherokee Nation. Severs undertook the task of erecting a building to house the new bank on land he claimed. At the corner of Broadway and Main, he put up a brick façade with the trademark slanted corner that marked many early bank buildings.

The First National Bank building was one of only a few brick or stone buildings in Muskogee at the time. Most were of wooden construction; many were described as little more than tarpaper shacks. These flimsy buildings made easy kindling when a fire broke out in Muskogee in February of 1899. It spread quickly from Second and Court to Main and Broadway. Much of downtown Muskogee was reduced to ashes.

The bricks of the Severs Block were credited with slowing the spread of the fire enough to allow the beleaguered firemen to finally get control of the blaze. Ironically over 100 years later, a fire at the Severs Block once again caused problems for Muskogee's downtown. Much of the interior of the old building was destroyed, but those bricks held the fire and kept it from spreading just as it had in 1899.

Death of Judge Parker Ended Era in Law Enforcement

For many people in Indian Territory and Muskogee, the death of Judge Isaac Parker in November of 1896 was a sad day. Though he had gained a reputation as a hard, unyielding dispenser of justice, for the people of Indian Territory, he had been a friend.

Parker had been appointed to the Western District of Arkansas in 1875 just three years after Muskogee was born. This court, at Fort Smith, was given jurisdiction over Indian Territory. The territory had gone from a relatively peaceful place before the Civil War, to one of vicious lawlessness when many outlaw gangs had moved into the territory to escape the jurisdiction of the surrounding states.

Parker had set out to tame this troubled frontier. He hired a virtual army of deputy marshals to scour Indian Territory of the criminal element. And he prosecuted these criminals to the fullest extent of the law, sentencing over 170 men to the death penalty. Nearly 80 convicted men were hanged during Parker's 21 years on the bench. It earned him the nickname of the "Hanging Judge."

Family members later related to his biographers that Parker disliked the appellation. He had not hanged these men, he said, "It is the law that has done it." Those who knew Parker personally said he was a gentle and kind man, but one with a strong sense of justice.

He had his share of critics, but most were people who did not live in Indian Territory and had not experienced the terror of uncontrolled crime. Most people along the rivers approved of Parker's firm hand in dealing with the outlaws.

Parker's grandson, also named Isaac Parker, related an experience he had some years after the judge's death. Young Parker had paid a business call on a blacksmith in Muskogee. After he introduced himself, the man asked if he was related to the famous "hanging judge." Parker confirmed that he was his grandson, fearing that the man might have had an experience in the judge's court. As it turned out the man's brother had been convicted of peddling whiskey. "It was the best thing that ever happened to my brother," the blacksmith said. "He came out of prison a changed man."

When news of Judge Parker's death was announced, those prisoners awaiting trial in his court were greatly relieved, believing they would receive a lighter sentence from someone else. But for the citizens of Fort Smith, Muskogee and other territory towns, it was a sad day. Many gathered in tribute to the man who had almost single handedly turned the tide of lawlessness in Indian Territory.

Deputy Marshal Built His Reputation on Integrity and a Quick Draw

Before the Emancipation Proclamation freed slaves in the South, the Creek Nation was apparently a known safe haven for escaping slaves from nearby states. According to oral tradition handed down among Freedmen descendants, Creek leaders refused to allow bounty hunters to enter their nation to capture escaped slaves. Nor would they return such individuals found within their borders.

This may be why an escaped slave named Bass Reeves made his way from Texas and spent a few years living in the Creek Nation. While hiding in Indian Territory, Reeves learned the Muscogee language and the lay of the land.

Following emancipation, Reeves settled on a farm near Van Buren, Arkansas, married and started a family. From time to time, he earned extra money acting as a scout and tracker for lawmen.

Following the Civil War, the Indian Territory had become a haven for criminals fleeing federal jurisdiction. In 1875, the federal court in Van Buren (later moved to Fort Smith) was given jurisdiction over Indian Territory.

Judge Isaac Parker was determined to clean up the region and recruited Bass Reeves and nearly 200 other men as deputy U.S. marshals. Parker had particularly sought African Americans for the service and it is believe Bass Reeves was the first black deputy marshal to be sworn to duty west of the Mississippi.

Reeves quickly established his reputation as a fearless lawman whose quick draw saved his life on many occasions. Known for his courteous manners and strict sense of duty, the marshal spent 32 years in the service and was responsible for nearly 3,000 arrests.

When a federal court was established in Muskogee in 1889, Reeves moved to Indian Territory and took up residence for a time in quarters near the federal jail.

Along with other marshals such as Bud Ledbetter, Reeves often found his duties involved enforcing the law that made it a crime to produce or sell alcohol in Indian Territory. Though the territory had been "dry" for years, the illegal sale of alcohol had always existed. "Busting" up stills and arresting those who brought whiskey into the Indian Nations kept the federal marshals busy. Bass Reeves was dogged in his determination to end the "bootlegging" that went on in Indian Territory. In fact, it was probably here that the term "bootleg" whiskey began. Moonshiners would slip the thin flasks of alcohol into the leg of their boots to bring it into the Indian Nations.

Reeves continued as a deputy marshal until Oklahoma statehood in 1907. At that time he went to work for the Muskogee Police Department. Even at age 69, his reputation as a lawman was so intimidating that crime was nonexistent on his beat.

Bass Reeves died in 1910 and was lauded in memorials as one of the greatest lawmen to have served in Indian Territory.

Lawmen, Cool Under Fire, Earned Tough Reputation

One of the longer-serving U.S. deputy marshals in Muskogee was Ernest Hubbard. He continued to receive appointments to serve as a deputy marshal even as the chief U.S. Marshal changed every four years or so.

Hubbard was often referred to as the chief office deputy and earned a reputation of being cool under fire. He frequently was chosen as the officer to escort convicted criminals to the federal prison in Leavenworth, Kansas.

One incident involving Hubbard occurred in March of 1907 in Muskogee. An organization calling itself the United Socialists had formed and declared themselves above the law and answerable to no governing authority. These anarchists (they might be called terrorists today) occupied a house on North Fourth Street and were heavily armed.

The owner of the home wanted them off his property and filed an eviction notice. When a Muskogee police officer named John Cofield went to the house to serve the notice, its occupants opened fire.

News of the shooting quickly reached Marshal Leo Bennett's office and he dispatched four deputies to the scene – Ernest Hubbard, Bud Ledbetter, Paul Williams and Paul Smith. When the officers arrived, they were immediately fired upon and they returned fired.

In the melee, over 50 shots were fired, but none of the marshals suffered an injury despite being out in the open street without cover. The house itself was riddled with bullets and several of the anarchists were either killed or wounded.

The shootout was naturally the talk of Muskogee for days afterward. It was one more incident that earned marshals such as Hubbard and also Bud Ledbetter their reputation of tough and unflinching in standing against the criminal element in Indian Territory.

So fearsome was their reputation that in another instance, combatants laid down their weapons before the marshals even arrived. Tensions were running high in Boynton and the town constable had wired Marshal Bennett for assistance. Bennett responded by wire that he was sending Hubbard and Ledbetter. When the deputies arrived, they made arrests without the need to fire a shot.

Often the outlaws of our wild and wooly past receive the attention and acclaim in books and movies. But the lawmen of Indian Territory were the true heroes and were highly respected by the grateful citizens of their day.

A Lack of Money Didn't Mean a Lack of Commerce

For many years in our history, even well into the Depression years of the 1930s, bartering for goods and services was a common practice. In the early days of Oklahoma's settlement, trade was conducted almost entirely on the barter system. There were no banks in Indian Territory until 1890 and little currency in circulation. None of the Indian tribes issued their own money so residents of the Territory often found coin to be scarce.

But that didn't stop commerce or trade in any way. The early mercantile business generally worked on two basic principals – bulk merchandise offered on extended credit. On the frontier, fur traders and farmers would visit the merchant only a few times a year. They wanted the goods they purchased in bulk quantities – barrels of meal, sacks of seed, or bolts of fabric. And they would want to keep a credit account and pay up once a year when the harvest was in.

This was the way early merchants in the Three Rivers region did business for years. Area residents would bring furs, wild turkey, venison and corn to exchange for merchandise at stores owned by Frederick Severs, James Hall, C.E. Foley and Clarence Turner. Local farmers would also pledge cattle and hogs on credit.

Many early merchants, including Severs and H.B. Spaulding became cattle ranchers because they were paid with cattle for the goods they carried. One of Clarence Turner's early responsibilities in his father's store in Okmulgee was to go out and collect those animals in the spring. The Turners would then herd their cattle into Muskogee and ship them to Kansas City or St. Louis on the Katy Railroad.

Bartering wasn't just for goods either. Services such as a haircut, or horse shoeing or a doctor's house call would also be paid on the barter system. Doctors almost always kept a chicken coop at their home for they were frequently paid with chickens for their services.

Ministers at local churches often lived on the tithes of vegetables from their parishioners' gardens as well as donations of milk, butter, cheese and eggs. And when the barber and the blacksmith traded services rather than goods, the fact that cash was scarce didn't seem to matter.

Even education used the barter system. Except for some tribal schools, education in Indian Territory was by subscription, meaning parents paid tuition for their children to attend school. As late as 1898, Henry Kendall College in Muskogee recorded on its books the receipt of everything from bales of hay to home-canned goods as payment for tuition.

In time the mercantiles became more like department stores and cash eventually replaced the barter system. Some stores, such as the Patterson Mercantile, even acted as early banks. Instead of having a credit account, customers would keep cash accounts with their small supply of money stored safely in the mercantile's big iron safe.

Folks on the frontier were often cash poor, but rich in the abundance of the harvest and the hunt. They found a way to amicably work around the lack of currency and commerce thrived around the Three Rivers.

Spaulding Left His Name on Muskogee's Landscape

H.B. Spaulding, for whom Spaulding Park in Muskogee is named, was an early-day businessman who moved to Muskogee from Sulphur Springs, Texas. He profited greatly from the tribal system of land use in Indian Territory. He married a Creek woman, Josephine Callahan, and this gave him access to Creek land. His ranch encompassed nearly 40 thousand acres on Cloud Creek between Muskogee and Checotah. His cattle herd numbered each year between 16 and 20 thousand head in the late 1890s.

Spaulding is said to have been the first person in Muskogee to own an automobile. According to the later remembrances of Tookah Turner, Spaulding's auto was called a White Steamer, possibly one manufactured by the Stanley Steamer Company.

Spaulding was proud of his auto and liked spinning around town to show it off. He once drove it to a picnic being held on the bank of the Arkansas River east of town. When Spaulding prepared to drive home, the car got stuck in reverse and almost landed him in the river. Spaulding had to back the car all the way home.

Homer and Josephine were strong supporters of the Methodist "Rock Church" and rebuilt the school associated with it after it was destroyed by fire. The school, first called Harrell Institute, was then named Spaulding Institute after its generous benefactors. The street in the front of the school was called Spaulding Boulevard. Eventually the name also would be applied to the park that developed between Spaulding Boulevard, G Street, Okmulgee Avenue and Park Drive.

When Spaulding came to Muskogee in 1884, he went to work at the Patterson Mercantile. Eventually he established his own store with a partner, W.S. Harsha.

Spaulding Mercantile also provided banking services to the cattlemen, farmers and other settlers in the area.

These merchants allowed people to keep cash in the store safe because of the lawlessness and theft that was common in Indian Territory. Eventually the mercantiles offered loans, accepted deposits, kept records of accounts, and made payments for individuals on their own checks. Spaulding issued his own paper notes, known by locals as "Spaulding scrip." Customers used it primarily to purchase goods in the Spaulding store, but other businesses around town accepted it for payments as well.

Spaulding was a true Muskogee supporter and served as mayor of the community in 1902. He promoted tourism and convention business for the city and later went on to serve as president of the Commercial Club, the organization that became the Chamber of Commerce.

The wealthy businessman applied his civic mindedness to the public's benefit when he built a steel bridge across the Arkansas River between Muskogee and Wagoner Counties in 1910. The piers of the long-gone bridge can still be seen from the current bridge on Highway 69.

First School Superintendent Had Enormous Job

Indian Territory's early schools were a patchwork system set up by the various tribes and by different mission organizations and churches. Schools were segregated from the beginning often even separating boys and girls.

Schools for Native American students were the first to be established by mission organizations. Some, such as the Union Mission near Mazie, operated as early as the 1820s. By the 1840s the Five Tribes had established schools for their own tribal members. Mission schools continued to develop throughout the Three Rivers region.

Following the Civil War, some of these mission schools began to teach the children of freedmen members of the tribes. But schools for children who were not tribal members were scarce at first. As towns began to develop along the rail lines in the 1870s, and more and more settlers moved into Indian Territory, the need for schools for their children became acute.

In towns subscription schools were started. Parents could pay a "subscription" or tuition for their children to attend. In rural areas, education was often neglected. Children were either schooled at home, walked for miles to the nearest subscription school, or received no education at all. Most of the schools were one-room buildings with teachers who themselves had often received only a limited education.

In 1898, with the passage of the Curtis Act, towns in Indian Territory could finally incorporate, elect a city government, raise taxes and establish public services including schools. The Curtis Act also transferred oversight of Indian Territory schools away from the tribes to the Interior Department. Interior Secretary, Ethan Allan Hitchcock, appointed John D. Benedict, an educator from Illinois, as superintendent of schools for all of Indian Territory. He arrived in Muskogee in February 1899 to begin the enormous task of bringing Indian Territory schools into a uniform public education system.

While the residents of Indian Territory were proud of the strides they had made in education since the passage of the Curtis Act, Benedict felt there was much room for improvement. However, he met with resistance from the tribes and so he spent his first months in Indian Territory traveling among the nations and getting acquainted with education leaders.

Benedict felt that one of the most effective ways to

improve public education in the territory would be to provide better teacher training. Working with Benjamin Coppock, appointed superintendent of Cherokee schools and Alice Robertson, superintendent of Creek schools, Benedict began summer training courses for teachers.

In the Cherokee Nation, the first teaching course was held at the Cherokee Female Seminary in Tahlequah in June 1900. The summer school brought a noticeable improvement in Cherokee schools so the following summer, the course was opened to any teacher in the territory who would like to attend. Benedict was especially interested in seeing teachers from the rural subscription schools be able to receive further training.

These teacher training schools continued each summer until Oklahoma became a state in 1907. Then schools passed from federal supervision to the state. The Cherokee Female Seminary had established itself as a teacher training facility and would eventually become Northeastern State University.

Railroad Day Celebrated New Roads

In 1904, the citizens of Muskogee held a celebration they called Railroad Day. The event brought thousands of visitors from the Three Forks area and beyond into the city. Muskogeeans were celebrating the arrival to their town of another railroad – the Midland Valley Railroad which had just completed the line it had begun in Hartford, Arkansas. This brought the fourth railroad to Muskogee and the town leaders realized that their community was rapidly becoming the railroad hub for Indian Territory.

The various railroads crisscrossing Muskogee offered discounted rates to travelers for that first Railroad Day held on May 18. People poured into the city and spent the day enjoying all types of festivities. Music was provided by the Merchant's Band, a group of amateur musicians who performed for the many parades and holidays that were held in Muskogee.

A great attraction for visitors was taking short excursion trips on the Muskogee Union and Midland Valley lines. And they were fascinated with the drilling of an oil well southeast of town. The local eateries reported serving lunch to 4,000 visitors that day.

In the afternoon, the crowd gathered at Henry Kendall College to watch a baseball game between the "Muskogee First Nine" and a team made of up of players from Pryor Creek and Vinita. Muskogee won by a score of 5 to 3. In the evening railroad dignitaries met at the Elks Club for a dinner hosted by the Muskogee Chamber of Commerce. Here railroad developer Charles Haskell was honored by the citizens for his efforts in bringing the Midland Valley Railroad to Muskogee. He was presented with a solid silver tea service.

The Midland Valley not only had chosen to lay track through Muskogee but was also going to build a depot, locate its headquarters in the city and constructs its shops here as well. This was a great economic boon for the city for a railroad headquartered here would employ hundreds of people.

From Muskogee, the Midland Valley Railroad continued to lay track westward following the route of the Arkansas River toward Tulsa. Along the way it connected or created towns such as Twine (now Taft), Haskell, Stone Bluff, Bixby and Jenks.

When the Midland Valley reached the Choska Bottoms, the towns of Sawokla and Ridge decided to pick up and move away from the Arkansas River and settle on the new rail line. Thus a new town was born in June 1904 and its residents chose to name it for the man most responsible for bringing the Midland Valley Railroad their way. They named the town Haskell in honor of Charles N.

Haskell, the railroad entrepreneur and first governor of Oklahoma.

The Midland Valley reached Tulsa by November 1904 and there crossed the Arkansas River and moved northward toward Kansas. When the railroad was completed it connected Fort Smith, Arkansas with Wichita, Kansas and hundreds of passengers a day traveled through Muskogee. Mr. Haskell had predicted on that first Railroad Day in 1904 that the way to build a great state was to build more railroads and he did exactly that.

Muskogee's Hinton Theater Hosted Many Historic Events

Even when Muskogee was still a dusty frontier town, its citizens had the opportunity to enjoy some excellent entertainment. Being located approximately halfway between Kansas City and Dallas, many traveling acting troupes and bands made a stop in Muskogee en route to these two cities. In the early days of statehood people from Tulsa would drive to Muskogee for their entertainment.

At first, any building with a large hall could serve as a location for a vaudeville act or a theater troupe. But in the late 1890s, Clarence Turner created an "opera house" over his hardware store at Main and Broadway. A truly elegant facility, the Turner Opera House hosted many fine productions before it was destroyed in the fire of 1899.

The growing city felt its need of a first class theater so in 1904 a St. Louis investor named G.H. Johnson proposed to build a theater at the corner of Third and Court Streets. To finance the construction, citizens of Muskogee sold seating for the opening event at $10 per seat. This raised $10,000 – a princely sum in 1904. The theater was completed the following year and named the Hinton Theater after a well-known entertainment entrepreneur named William Hinton.

In August of 1905, the Hinton hosted the Sequoyah State Convention. Here representatives from Indian Territory met to draft a constitution for a state separate from Oklahoma Territory. Creek Chief Pleasant Porter was elected president of the convention and two future governors, Charles Haskell and William Murray were delegates to the convention. Citizens of Indian Territory approved the Sequoyah Constitution the following November, but Congress declined to act on it, instead passing the Enabling Act to combine the Twin Territories into the State of Oklahoma.

The Hinton continued for many years to be Muskogee's most impressive theater. Fred Turner bought the opera house in 1920 and spent $150,000 remodeling it. He renamed it the Orpheum Theater and ushered in the motion picture. Later George Procter and Hugh Marsh took over the theater and renamed it the Ritz. The Ritz Theater, as its name implies, was Muskogee's finest. Procter and Marsh introduced "talkies" – movies with sound – and continued to book vaudeville acts and road shows.

In 1926, Will Rogers performed at the Orpheum to a packed audience who didn't want the show to end. Rogers, with his home-spun humor and fancy rope tricks, pulled a trick on the audience. He stepped from the stage onto the piano in the orchestra pit and kept talking. Then he proceeded down the aisle, talking all the while, until he slipped out the front door.

The Ritz Theater enjoyed many years of success, but like all the other downtown theaters finally gave way to the multiplex theaters and the malls. Today, only the Roxy Theater, another Procter and Marsh property, still stands in Muskogee's historic downtown.

7

Oklahoma's First Century

Trans-Mississippi Congress Hosted by Muskogee in 1907

On what is now a parking lot for the federal building in downtown Muskogee once stood Convention Hall, a building constructed for the purpose of hosting the Trans-Mississippi Congress. A group of Muskogee businessmen, mostly bankers, had financed the construction of the building that took up the city block between Main and Second Streets.

The Trans-Mississippi Congress was a regional commercial club whose purpose was to promote commerce and development west of the Mississippi River. It was organized in 1891 and held a convention each year in various western cities such as St. Louis, Denver, Seattle and San Francisco.

At the 1906 convention in Kansas City, A.C. Trumbo attended as a delegate from Muskogee. He introduced a bid to have his hometown host the convention the following year. Since Oklahoma was about to become a state, there was a great interest in the region. Muskogee received a unanimous vote to host the convention in 1907.

There was one problem with Trumbo's plan, however. Muskogee did not have a building large enough to house such a gathering. One would have to be built. So Trumbo, along with his father-in-law Augustus Patterson, led the crusade to get a building up in time for the convention to be held November 19-22, 1907. At a cost of $40,000, the building could seat five thousand people. The main entrance was on the second floor and was accessed by stairs from Second Street.

For the event, Muskogeeans developed a special cheer for the city. This was at the request of Charles Madison the president of the One Hundred Thousand Club. This organization had set a goal to see Muskogee's population reach 100,000 by 1910. The city's population was 22,000 at the time.

The four-day Congress brought thousands of visitors to Muskogee, including the Chinese Ambassador to the United States and several governors of western states and territories. Thirty passenger trains a day arrived in Muskogee for that week, bringing delegates from all over the west.

Navigation on the Arkansas River was the main topic of interest at the Congress. It was opposed by the railroads which realized water transportation would bring competition and drive freight costs down. Other cities, such as Oklahoma City, also opposed the idea of Arkansas navigation, fearing it would give cities such as Muskogee an advantage in attracting industry.

Convention Hall continued to host many of Muskogee's largest events for years after the Trans-Mississippi Congress. Boxing matches and other sporting events were held there as well as the annual fireman's ball. Ironically, the building was destroyed by fire in 1957.

Planes and Trucks Were Once Manufactured in Okay

While Okay, Oklahoma would never rival Detroit for automobile production, it did make quite a mark on the automotive industry with the O-K Truck. This sturdy product proved to be a popular model following World War I.

The O-K Truck was manufactured in a rock building that had been constructed of native sandstone in 1907. It was built to be a meat packing plant for the cattle ranches in the area, but never actually served that purpose. It stood empty and uncompleted near the little town of Rex (an early name for Okay) until 1910 when a Mr. McDaniel from Ohio bought it, finished the building and began a stove manufacturing business there. Rex Stoves were produced from 1910 to 1912. Following that, plows were manufactured at the plant until 1915.

The Oklahoma Auto Manufacturing Company acquired the building and moved into it in 1916. Production of trucks began that year and continued through the 1920s. The company employed 100 men and turned out about three trucks a day. They produced a 1-ton, 1 ½-ton and 2-ton truck. The 1-ton model was a four-cylinder, 29.8 horsepower truck with a three-speed transmission. The trucks had solid rubber tires and wheels with wooden spokes. The cost on the trucks averaged $1,295.

The O-K Trucks were completely assembled at the Okay plant except for the engine which was manufactured elsewhere. The trucks sold well throughout the country. In fact, business boomed right after World War I. In 1919, the plant was so busy it fell behind in meeting orders and buyers would come to Okay to save time in delivery of the trucks. Dealerships for the truck were located throughout the Midwest and even as far as the West Coast.

By the late 1920s, however, the economy was slowing and truck sales fell off. The company floundered in financial difficulties and finally went out of business in 1927. Several unfinished trucks were parked in a field near the sandstone building until they were finally sold for scrap. But the O-K Trucks on the road kept running. They were so well built that they continued to be used as a farm and oilfield workhorse until the 1940s.

After auto manufacturing ended, the rock building was converted to an airplane factory for a brief period. It produced a monoplane with two open cockpits. The plane had a wingspan of 26 feet and was fabric covered. It was powered by a five-cylinder radial engine with 110 horsepower. The fuselage was welded steel tubing and the wings had spruce spars.

In all, only three planes were ever built at the Okay plant. An O-K Truck towed the first plane that was produced out to a nearby pasture for a test flight in 1928. The wings had to be mounted on the plane out in the pasture. The test flight drew quite a crowd – people lined the road to watch the event.

But before the business itself could get off the ground, the Wall Street Crash of 1929 brought everything to a halt. The Okay Airplane Company went out of business that year. The building and all equipment of the company were sold. Ruins of the automotive/airplane factory still stand in Okay today.

Boy Scouting Has Early Roots in Oklahoma

In 1950, the Boy Scouts of America were celebrating their 40th anniversary, having been chartered by a Chicago businessman in 1910. A Boy Scout troop was begun in Muskogee that same year. But the first Scout troop in America was begun in Pawhuska, Oklahoma in

1909. This is probably why Oklahoma has many Scout troops whose beginnings date back to the founding of the Scouting movement.

The theme for their 40th anniversary was "Strengthen the Arm of Liberty" and a project adopted by Scout troops was to place little Statues of Liberty in small towns and large cities all across America. These statues are known today as the Little Sisters of Liberty. Nearly 200 of them were placed in parks, on main streets, and in front of city halls, courthouses and capitols in 39 states. Kansas can boast of having the most Little Liberties with 26. Oklahoma had at least 12 statues placed by the Boy Scouts in cities such as Tulsa and Oklahoma City and smaller towns like Lindsay and Tahlequah.

The idea of the Little Sisters of Liberty began with a Kansas City businessman who was the Scout Commissioner of that city's Area Council. J.P. Whitaker published a pamphlet describing the project and it caught on across the country. He wrote, "Americans, more than ever before, need to be reminded that freedom, like life itself, is preserved only through vigilance and care." A Chicago firm manufactured the copper statues that stand 8 feet, 4 inches tall. Each city was responsible for the base that the statue sits on so these vary from town to town.

Muskogee has its own Little Sister of Liberty located in Spaulding Park. The local Boy Scout troop raised the $300 needed to purchase the copper statue. The city provided an island pedestal and placed it in the center of the pond at the park. She has stood proudly in the park for most of the years since then.

Vandals damaged her lifted arm in 1978 and she was removed until 1982. Parks director, Henry Bresser, and a park crew restored Little Liberty at that time, drained and cleaned the pond, restocked it with fish and then reinstated the statue to her rightful place.

A renewed interest in the Little Sisters of Liberty began after the terrorist attack on America on September 11, 2001. Tony Rajer, a conservator who has restored several of the statues was quoted in an article in *American Profile* magazine. "The statue is symbolic of all that the terrorists wanted to destroy," he said. "They didn't destroy it."

If you look closely at the Liberty statue in Spaulding Park, you will notice that the face truly is of a little sister. It is the face of a young girl, rather than being an exact replica of the world-famous Lady who stands in New York Harbor.

These mass-produced statues are not considered great art – but they represent America's great values. Muskogee should be proud of its Little Sister of Liberty and the freedom and patriotism she represents.

Courageous Woman Inspired a Town

Many towns in Oklahoma have nearly faced extinction at some time in their history due to fire, flood or tornado. Some towns never recover from a disaster and become little more than ghost towns at the end of dirt roads, just a shadowed reminder of their former selves. Other towns are inspired to fight back after a devastating loss to rebuild and keep their town alive.

The town of Webbers Falls had to rebuild more than once in its long history. This community, named for the Cherokee leader Walter Webber, was established early in the state's history, gaining a post office in 1856. Its residents witnessed the conflict of the Civil War as few towns in Indian Territory did. Union forces practically wiped out the town with fire in 1863.

But its Cherokee citizens returned after the war and rebuilt the river town where steamboats frequently stopped to wait for higher water levels to make it over the falls on the Arkansas River. The little town prospered and developed a thriving downtown of mercantiles and cotton gins.

Then on March 11, 1911, fire once again threatened the town. A clerk at the Hayes Mercantile stepped into the back warehouse for an item and glanced out the window. A blaze whipped by strong winds was already engulfing much of the downtown district. There was little time to take action to fight the fire.

In one of the downtown buildings, a nineteen-year-old telephone operator named Rose Coppinger was working at the town's central switchboard. In those days all calls were still handled through a local switchboard and the operator generally knew everyone in town.

Young Rose stayed at her switchboard despite the smoke, heat and flames and calmly but quickly warned residents about the fire. One by one she connected to telephones throughout the town to let people know of the danger so they could flee the flames. Though others urged her to leave her post, she would not do so until she had made contact with everyone she could. Rose had to be carried from the burning building wrapped in a wet blanket to make it through the inferno.

Despite Rose's efforts, most of the downtown was destroyed, but no lives were lost. Most homes were spared when firefighters made a stand at the Hayes Mercantile and finally got the flames under control there. Several stores, two banks, restaurants, drug stores, cotton gins and pool halls were all gone in a matter of hours.

The citizens of Webbers Falls were inspired by the courage of Rose Coppinger. They petitioned and won for her a Carnegie Medal for Heroism and took up a collection totally $500 as a token of their esteem. Since Rose had lost what belongings she had in the burned building, this act of gratitude was a great blessing to her.

Businessmen in Webbers Falls met at the Hayes Mercantile the evening after the fire. With Rose's courage fresh in their minds, they each one vowed to rebuild their businesses. Tents were set up in town until new buildings could be erected. Surveyors came the following week and laid out new streets. Webbers Falls, inspired by a young woman's courage, turned tragedy into triumph over adversity to rise again.

Jefferson Highway Among Earliest Interstate Roads

In 1914, Henry Ford began producing his Model T on the assembly line. This brought the price of a car down to about $300 and put it within almost everyone's reach. Suddenly America was able to travel like it never had before. And this created a need for good roads.

Some roads, like the Texas Road through the Three Rivers region, had been so well traveled for so long that they were wide and hard packed. Travel along such routes was relatively easy except in very rainy or snowy conditions. But most roads throughout America, except for the cities, were simple dirt wagon tracks, difficult for automobiles to travel and impossible for any mode of transportation when wet and muddy. Thus a "good roads movement" began in 1914 and civic and municipal organizations began working on the need for better roads.

E.T. Meredith, editor of *Better Homes and Gardens* magazine in 1915, proposed the formation of highway to run through the states that were part of the Louisiana Purchase. Meredith thought the road should be called the Jefferson Highway in honor of Thomas Jefferson's "greatest real estate deal in history" in 1803. A call went out to the states making up the Louisiana Purchase to meet in New Orleans in November 1915 to discuss such a highway. D.N. Fink, president of Commercial National Bank of Muskogee, attended as a delegate from the youngest state, Oklahoma.

Out of that and subsequent meetings evolved the Jefferson Highway Association with the goal of building a "365-day road" (meaning it could be traveled even in wet weather). The main cities along this highway were to be New Orleans, Baton Rouge, Denison, Muskogee, Joplin, Kansas City, Des Moines, St. Paul and Winnipeg, Manitoba. The route veered out of the Louisiana Purchase in that neither Texas nor Manitoba had been part of that great land deal. This was necessary in part, because in 1915 western Arkansas had no roads.

The Jefferson Highway Association raised funds for the project by membership dues of $9 per mile. Many counties also raised funds for the road through bond issues. So the road was a cooperative effort between government and private enterprise.

As early as 1916 a relay "sociability run" was made along a portion of the "Pine to Palm" road as it was being called. Nearly 500 cars took part in this effort to advertise the road and build cooperation between the communities along the route. Oklahoma was doing its part in getting the highway built, following the route of the Texas Road. D.N. Fink, who had been elected vice president of the Jefferson Highway Association, reported in 1916 that he and his family had traveled from Muskogee to Joplin (149 miles) in "just seven hours."

In 1925, highway commissioners from 11 states in the Mississippi Valley met at Kansas City to work on plans to bring state roads into a numbered federal highway system. The Jefferson Highway, being one of the best in America at that time, was made a federal highway. The Oklahoma portion of this road was designated U.S. Highway 69.

Road construction was delayed during WWI but it was projected that by 1929 the entire 2,300 miles of the Jefferson Highway would be paved, beating Route 66 which wasn't completed until 1938. The Jefferson Highway Association marked the entire route with blue and white directional poles and aggressively advertised it as a "tourist's delight." In Muskogee, the Kiwanis Club built a tourist camp at Spaulding Park that could accommodate 200 cars and camps were also built at Miami, Pryor, Eufaula and McAlester.

Baseball Bests the Courtroom Any Day

District Judge Enloe Verner was born in Elkhorn, Illinois in 1879. He attended law school at Washington University, graduating in 1904. Since his hometown already had a number of established lawyers, he thought he would head west and look for opportunity for a young man just starting out. He first visited Rosebud, South Dakota, but didn't find much opportunity there.

So he returned to St. Louis and bought a ticket on the KATY Flyer heading to Galveston, Texas. His ticket allowed two stopovers on the journey and he made his first stop at Muskogee. He looked the town over and liked what he saw of Indian Territory's most progressive city in 1904. He decided to stay and never used the rest of his ticket.

In October 1904, Verner took his bar examination at the U.S. Courthouse, then located in the Railway Exchange Building. After a couple of anxious days waiting for the results, he learned he had passed the exam and his license was issued.

Verner ran for county judge in 1916 and then in 1922 sought the district judgeship where he served for a number of years. When applying for admission to practice before the Supreme Court, Verner visited the Washington D.C. office of Congresswoman Alice Robertson. Miss Robertson asked if she could accompany him to the Supreme Court to be presented. Verner later said he considered that one of the great honors of his career.

Being a judge, of course, has some very serious moments, but there can be some embarrassing ones as well. During an interview with the *Muskogee Times-Democrat* in 1940, Judge Verner recalled his most embarrassing moment.

At this time the court met in the Metropolitan Building located at the corner of 4th and Okmulgee. Judge Verner's courtroom and offices overlooked the Muskogee baseball park across the street. He had a good view of afternoon ball games; in fact, he could even hear the umpire call the balls and strikes.

On this particular day, Muskogee's minor league team was within a game or so of leading the league. The game being played was a close one. Judge Verner was trying to hear arguments in a civil case that was proving to be dry and uninteresting. The judge was sitting at his bench at a side angle so he could see the ballpark. He was pretending to listen to the attorneys, but his mind was on the game outside.

They were in the ninth inning and the score was close. Muskogee had two men on base and a batter who had not been doing very well was coming up to bat. By this time, Judge Verner was giving little attention to the court proceedings. He said, "I saw the batter swing hard and I saw the ball sail clear out of the field. Before I knew what I was doing I yelled, 'He knocked a homerun!'"

Immediately Judge Verner realized he had said this out loud! The attorney who had been presenting his case had a pained expression on his face, but everyone else in the courtroom was laughing loudly. Judge Verner attempted to apologize, but to little avail. He said, "Somehow I couldn't rap for silence."

Judge Verner had a long illustrious career in Muskogee, but he never forgot his most embarrassing moment.

Annual Girl Scout Cookie Sales Began in Muskogee

Few things are as comfortably predictable as the annual ritual of Girl Scout cookie sales. Who of us can resist the fresh, freckled smiles of girls offering shortbreads and thin mints and a dozen or so other delectable confections? And where did this great American cookie sale get started? In Muskogee, Oklahoma.

It was December 1917 during the difficult days of World War I. The local Girl Scout troop, known as the Mistletoe Troop, was looking for a unique service project. What they settled upon was baking sugar cookies in their mothers' kitchens, then wrapping them in wax paper and taking them to the Central High School cafeteria to sell. The cookies were a hit and the Girl Scouts discovered a successful fundraiser that soon would sweep across the country.

In 1917, the Girl Scouts of America were still just a fledgling organization. The first Girl Scout troop had been established in 1912 in Savannah, Georgia by Juliette Gordon Low, whose nickname was Daisy. Under Daisy's guidance and with her financial support, soon Girl Scout troops were being organized across the country. The organization was incorporated in 1915 and began holding an annual convention at that time. When the Mistletoe Troop started in Muskogee is unclear, but they were obviously active and well organized by 1917.

In 1922, a recipe for shortbread cookies was published in a national scouting magazine and recommended as a fundraiser. Soon shortbread cookies and Girl Scouts were almost synonymous. Throughout the 1920s and 1930s, the Scouts baked the cookies at home, wrapped them by the dozen, and sold them door to door for 25 cents. During World War II, the Girl Scouts turned to other fundraisers because of shortages of sugar, flour and butter. But after the war, cookie sales were resumed, this time with professional bakers vying for the chance to be licensed Girl Scout cookie producers.

Muskogee's troop was very active in the 1920s as well. They held a large rally in 1920 with Mrs. Ernest Thompson Seton, wife of the founder of the Boy Scouts, as their special guest. A service project undertaken by the girls in 1921 was to offer child care at the Oklahoma Free State Fair where nearly 10,000 visitors a day were recorded.

In 1922, the Girl Scouts helped in Muskogee's efforts to host the national Rotary Convention that brought thousands of Rotarians to the city.

Celebrated History Scholar has Roots in Rentiesville

The town of Rentiesville was established by William Rentie in 1905 on the freedman allotments of the Rentie family. It was one of several all-black towns created in the Three Rivers area after allotment, and it flourished in the days of segregation. Buck Franklin, a lawyer of Chickasaw and African American heritage, settled his family there, established his legal practice and served as justice of the peace.

His son John was born in Rentiesville in 1915 and he spent the first ten years of his life in this quiet McIntosh County town. Surrounded by this community of color, John had little experience with the injustices of segregation in his early life. But at age seven, an experience would change his perception of the world and set his course in trying to change that world.

The Franklins would often travel to Checotah to do their shopping and one day in 1922, they flagged a Katy train passing through Rentiesville. Climbing aboard the passenger train, they entered a car that was reserved for whites. John's parents felt very strongly that they must never voluntarily submit to segregation. So Mrs. Mollie Franklin, John and his sister took a seat in the car. When the conductor told them they would have to leave the car, Mrs. Franklin refused. So the conductor stopped the train and put them off. They had to walk back to Rentiesville.

John Hope Franklin points to this moment as a pivotal one in his life. He would face other incidences of segregation and racism, but this one stirred the first embers of his determination to stand against prejudice and injustice.

The Franklins moved to Tulsa in 1925 because Buck Franklin found it difficult to make a living in little Rentiesville. John graduated from Booker T. Washington High School as its valedictorian and went on to further his education at Fisk University in Tennessee. He intended to pursue a degree in law and return to Tulsa to join his father's law firm. But a history professor at Fisk stirred another passion in John and he instead went on to Harvard to get his graduate degree in history.

For his thesis, John turned to a little studied aspect of American history – the history of African Americans. His research would later lead him to write *From Slavery to Freedom*, a book that has sold over 3 million copies and has been translated into several languages. John Hope Franklin introduced America to black history in a fair and dispassionate work that continues to be honored today.

Franklin also achieved his life-long goal at striking a blow against segregation. He served on the team of lawyers and scholars who assisted Thurgood Marshall in presenting the legal arguments against school segregation in the landmark Supreme Court case, *Brown vs. the Board of Education*.

Rentiesville native, John Hope Franklin, was recognized as the most celebrated American historian having been awarded 105 honorary degrees from colleges and universities around the world.

Cool-headed Leaders Kept Muskogee Bank from Failing in Crisis

Despite the chilly weather on February 10, 1926, people were gathering on the streets of downtown Muskogee. A rumor had begun to circulate throughout town that the Commercial National Bank was about to fail. Fueling these rumors was the recent failure of a bank in Stigler and the dismal state of agriculture in Muskogee County. Cotton prices were extremely depressed and the local economy was suffering.

When Commercial Bank officials opened their doors for business on that chilly Wednesday morning, they were met by customers waiting to get in. Fearful of losing their savings, small depositors had come to withdraw their funds from the bank. Within minutes, the line of customers stretched across the lobby and this only fueled speculation among townsfolk that something was amiss.

Trying to keep an air of calm, bank officials remained in their offices, going about business as usual in the hopes that this would reassure customers. It did not. The lines to the three teller windows kept growing as the day progressed. What was meant to look like calm businesslike behavior began to look like indifference or even ignorance. The mood of the crowd of customers changed from worry to anger.

Word of the bank run spread throughout Muskogee and the lines grew even longer, now stretching outside the bank at 3rd and Broadway and around the block. Spectators milled about and talked in hushed, worried tones. Small business owners watched out their windows downtown, caught in the drama taking place outside.

These business owners knew that a run on one bank could trigger runs on every bank in town. There was no Federal Deposit Insurance at that time. If other banks closed this would certainly bring complete ruin to the economy and would lead to their own business failures. Though many Muskogee business owners had accounts at Commercial, they all realized they must not give into the fearful frenzy by withdrawing their own funds. They would have to grit their teeth, sit tight, and hope that the crisis passed.

Members of the Retail Merchants Association and the Chamber of Commerce rallied around the bank, expressing support of the institution. Business owners were urged to make deposits to Commercial as a show of confidence. But by 1:30 that afternoon, the crowds were so thick in the bank lobby, no one could get inside to make a deposit.

At that time, Commercial National Bank president, D.N. Fink, stepped out of his office and mounted a marble railing in the lobby to speak to the people. He reassured them that the bank was solvent, but could not remain so if everyone withdrew their deposits. He went outside and spoke to the crowd on the street from the hood of an automobile, almost begging them to step back from the precipice over which the entire local economy might be swept.

The bank closed its doors at the normal time, still in business, but barely. More Muskogee leaders rallied to the bank's support. Local labor unions met and voted to keep their accounts at Commercial. That evening business leaders spoke during intermission at the movie theaters, urging people to stay calm and avoid pulling the bank under.

The Federal Reserve rushed cash funds to the bank by train overnight and this was reported in the *Phoenix* the next morning. The cooler heads prevailed and calm was restored. Commercial National Bank was soon reorganized with new officers and went on to become Muskogee's largest bank for a time.

WPA Left a Lasting Legacy in Three Rivers Region

During the Depression, when jobs were scarce and money was scarcer, the Works Progress Administration (WPA) gave jobs to thousands of people. The WPA is probably best known for the many native stone structures its workers built, but the agency actually took on projects in many different areas.

In the Three Rivers region, the WPA worked on many projects that still stand today. WPA workers built the dam, several cabins, and the lodge at Greenleaf State Park. Even some of the original WPA picnic tables still remain at the park today.

Near Sallisaw, the WPA restored the log cabin that had been the home of Sequoyah, the famed Cherokee who developed their written language. The WPA workers built a stone structure to enclose and protect the fragile old building. Closer to Muskogee, the WPA restored the Fort Gibson Stockade in the 1930s.

Local historian Grant Foreman had been instrumental in gaining the WPA's assistance on the restoration of Sequoyah's Cabin and the Fort Gibson

Stockade. Several other historical projects were also completed under Foreman's direction, with work provided by the WPA. These included collecting oral histories from local Native Americans and black Freedmen. He also oversaw the indexing of all the newspapers in the state at that time and other similar jobs that employed clerical workers and writers.

Several school structures in the Three Rivers area were built by WPA workers. Many of them are still standing and are used in some capacity today. These include buildings at Connors State College in Warner, the Wainwright school and gymnasium, Muskogee's Athletic Field and Stadium (Indian Bowl) and schools in Wagoner. In fact, Wagoner is rich in WPA buildings – the Armory, the County Courthouse, the City Hall and the community building were constructed by its workers.

And let's not forget a very significant work in Muskogee – Honor Heights Park, one of eastern Oklahoma's most popular tourist attractions. Though the park is known for its azaleas and Christmas lights, the beauty of the park is certainly enhanced by the waterfall, rock steps and pathways that meander around its hill. All were built by the WPA.

In fact nearly every small town in the Three Rivers region can point to at least one WPA project still in existence. A school, an armory, a lake or park, a street or sidewalk -- usually built with native stones or locally produced bricks -- can be found within the city limits of many a hometown. And because Oklahoma's WPA workers did such quality work, these rock-solid structures have stood the test of time and are still used, enjoyed and admired today.

Honor Heights Park Was the Most Beautiful in 1935

Honor Heights Park began when the city of Muskogee purchased 40 acres of land on Agency Hill in 1909. The city fathers of that day must have had a great deal of imagination and faith to see a park on that unclaimed hillside. At the time, it was simply an overgrown bramble of native trees and vines with only a narrow winding wagon trail clinging to the side of the hill. Its main attraction was that this trail provided a spectacular view of Muskogee, sprawling across the prairie below.

By the time the park was given its official name in 1919 to honor Muskogee area veterans of World War I, the hillside was beginning to take shape. Park Superintendent George Palmer, an English gardener from New York City, was by then laying out its gardens in the English cottage tradition.

In 1927, the Muskogee Chamber of Commerce had formed a "City Beautiful" Committee with the obvious task of working toward the beautification of Muskogee. From that group of dedicated volunteers grew the Muskogee Garden Club, which continues today. In 1935, the Garden Club voted to enter Honor Heights Park and the City of Muskogee in the *Better Homes and Gardens* "More Beautiful America" contest.

The reason for their pride was the tremendous amount of work that had been done in Honor Heights Park from 1930 when the Club formed to 1935 when they entered the contest. The City had been hard hit by the Depression like most areas of the country. Funds for maintaining the Park simply were not available. So the City applied for public works assistance from the state which ran a program similar to the WPA. With these state workers, the park that we know today took shape.

Under the supervision of the Garden Club, the natural rocks found in the park were used to create the waterfall that cascades down the side of Agency Hill. Mule teams were employed to haul the rocks and thousands of hours of arduous labor were involved. These rocks were also used to create walkways and build picnic tables and benches.

The underbrush was cleared and the trees were trimmed of low and dead branches. The wagon trail was graveled for automobile traffic. At a cost of $22.50, the Garden Club built the footbridge at the lower edge of the brook that meanders through the park.

The editor of *Better Homes and Gardens*, Elmer Peterson, visited Muskogee and was impressed with what he found in this clean and attractive city. Honor Heights Park and the City of Muskogee won the "More Beautiful America" contest that year.

Peterson wrote in the magazine, "I'm not merely enthusiastic but completely dumfounded at the things this city has done. [The park] was transformed from a towering jungle-wilderness of rock-strewn, weedy, unkempt terrain into a fairyland, adorned by acres of tree and shrub plantings, rock gardens, pools, flowers and shady walks and drives."

The *Better Homes and Gardens* editor went on to say, "If the park is maintained and reasonably developed, it will be a year-after-year mecca for American gardeners." Little did he know what Honor Height Park would become and what a source of pride it would continue to be for the city of Muskogee.

Floyd and Other Outlaws Used Cookson Hills as Refuge

Oklahoma received its reputation as an outlaw

haven back in its Indian Territory days when the law was restricted in making arrests on Indian land. Outlaw gangs such as the Doolins, the James Brothers, Belle Starr and Cherokee Bill had all found the Ozark foothills well suited to hiding from the law.

Depression era outlaws such as Charles "Pretty Boy" Floyd, Wilbur Underhill, and Bonnie and Clyde followed almost literally in their footsteps along the back roads of the hills and "hollers" of the Cookson Hills and other rural stretches of Oklahoma.

Floyd was born in Georgia but his family moved to Oklahoma when he was small so he grew up in Sequoyah County. Though he is usually associated with Oklahoma, much of his crime spree actually occurred outside the state. But he would return to the Oklahoma hills when he needed to lay low for awhile.

Floyd had a mixed reputation. He was often described as dapper and polite by the individuals he dealt with, even while robbing a bank or hijacking a car. But he also was known to be ruthless and quick on the trigger. He had served one short prison term and had vowed never to be sent back to jail. Folks knew if he was cornered he would come out shooting.

Like Belle Starr before him, Pretty Boy's legendary status probably exceeded his actual exploits. He was accused of crimes that he claimed he never committed. He did, however, rob the bank in Morris twice in the span of only a few months. And despite roadblocks set up in Okmulgee and Muskogee Counties, he managed to escape capture after each heist. The hills hid him and his crime partners well.

It is often reported that the rural folks around his favorite hideouts helped Floyd and his gang evade the law. In some cases this is probably true. Some folks admired their bank robberies because of their own negative experiences with banks. But just as often, people chose to look the other way rather than turn in such criminals as Floyd because they feared them. A criminal known to carry a machine gun around was not someone most folks wanted to cross.

The law finally caught up with Charles Floyd on a farm in Ohio. He was shot while trying to flee arrest. He had expressed to his mother a desire to be buried in Oklahoma so his body was returned to Sequoyah County. Thousands attended his funeral at the Akins Cemetery and the Ozark foothills became his final resting place.

Camp Gruber Brought War Effort Close to Home

America entered World War II following the bombing of Pearl Harbor in December 1941. Very soon afterward in January 1942, it was announced that an army training facility would be built in the Three Rivers area. The Cookson Hills would be the site of the camp, just 18 miles east of Muskogee near Braggs on Highway 10.

Named Camp Gruber, for Brigadier General Edmund Gruber, author of "The Caisson Song," the facility was under construction by February. Manhattan Construction Company of Muskogee, utilizing a workforce of 12,000, worked around the clock to complete over 2,000 buildings on the 260-acre site. The facility was completed by May 1942 at a cost of $30 million.

Camp Gruber was a small city in itself with 479 barracks, a two-mile parade ground, a hospital, post office and several social and recreational facilities. Bus service was available within the camp for five cents a ride and service was also available to nearby towns like Muskogee. A round-trip fare to Muskogee on the Victory Bus Line was 61 cents.

The training camp officially opened on May 21, 1942 with Colonel H.C. Luck as post commander. The first army division to begin training there was the 88th Infantry, called the "Cloverleaf" division since its days of service in World War I. Next the 202 Field Artillery began training at Gruber in October 1942.

The following spring in April 1943, President Franklin Roosevelt made a surprise visit to the base. He watched the 88th Infantry go through its drills on the parade ground and declared it "a wonderful show." He then ate dinner with the troops at the mess hall. The President came to Gruber to see the 88th because they were preparing for deployment. After nearly a year of training, they were shipping out to Fort Sam Houston in Texas and then on to Europe.

The 88th Infantry had an impressive record of service. As the first allied troops to enter Rome in June 1944, the 88th were in combat for 344 days and saw high casualties. Two Congressional Medals of Honor were awarded to men of the "Cloverleaf" division.

During the summer of 1943, a prisoner of war facility was added to Camp Gruber. At completion the camp had a capacity of 5,750 prisoners. The German captives were part of Field Marshal Erwin Rommel's Afrika Corp. The prisoners worked on farms in the area as well as in a nearby rock quarry.

Another infantry division, the 42nd, began training at Camp Gruber in July 1943. This division had been given the nickname the "Rainbow" Division by its most famous member, General Douglas McArthur. The 42nd deployed in November of 1944 to Camp Kilmer in New Jersey and then to Germany. The "Rainbow" Division liberated the Dachau concentration camp in Germany on April 29, 1945.

Muskogee residents opened their homes to the soldiers at Camp Gruber, inviting them to Sunday dinner after church and to Christmas and other holiday celebrations. When the troops shipped out for combat, the town would host a parade to see them to the train station. Townsfolk would line the streets, waving flags or handkerchiefs, offering encouragement and prayers for "our boys." It was hard to see them go, knowing many would not return.

To the people of the Three Rivers region, the World War II fighter was not a nameless, faceless soldier. He was someone they had sat across the dinner table from and had danced with at the USO. Camp Gruber gave northeastern Oklahoma a stake in the war that it might not otherwise have known.

Flood Washed WWII off Front Pages in 1943

News of the Allies fighting Japan in the Pacific was temporarily knocked off the front pages of newspapers in northeastern Oklahoma in the spring of 1943. For several days heavy rains in early May had drenched the Three Rivers region. The rain was welcomed by farmers, but when it just kept coming, flooding became a serious concern.

By May 11, rivers throughout the region were swollen beyond their banks and continuing to rise. This was before the extensive system of dams and reservoirs had been built on the Grand, Verdigris and Arkansas Rivers. There was nothing to stop the torrent of water draining into the Arkansas from its many tributaries.

Soldiers on a weekend pass to Tulsa could not return to Camp Gruber because highways were covered and bridges were closed. Their passes were extended until the floodwaters receded. Other soldiers from the 88th Division at Gruber were called into action to help rescue individuals who were stranded in trees and on rooftops. Using pontoon boats rigged with motors, the soldiers had to assist in evacuating the entire town of Webbers Falls.

Bottom lands along the rivers were inundated and it is estimated the Arkansas between Muskogee and Fort Gibson was nine miles wide at the height of flooding and the waters crested at over 48 feet, some 20 feet above flood stage. Levees along the river had huge holes torn into them. Muskogee's water supply was cut off for days.

Several soldiers were thrown from a boat as they worked to rescue people in Haskell County. Four soldiers were drowned in this incident, as well as two civilians. One soldier who survived the dunk in the river was carried all the way to Fort Smith before he could be rescued.

Because of these soldiers' deaths, when flooding again threatened in the spring of 1945, a mandatory evacuation was ordered. Everyone living within flood prone areas was given only a short time to pack up what belongings they could in a vehicle or wagon and move to higher ground. That year, German prisoners of war housed at Camp Gruber, also assisted with cleanup after the storms.

Veteran Was Part of America's Best Division in World War II

Charles L. Kilgore, a Muskogee Central High School student back in 1936, considered himself lucky to be able to serve in the Oklahoma National Guard where he received one day's pay for just two hours of work at the armory each week. At that time, one day's pay was 97 cents for a buck private.

Kilgore had been able to sign up with the Guard at the age of 15 because he was big for his age and assumed to be older than he was. He was part of the medical detachment of the 180th Infantry at Muskogee. It took him six months to work up the courage to tell his parents that he had joined the service.

He attended summer camp at Fort Sill and was promoted to Private First Class at the end of the camp. He served three more years in the medical corp., then attended a semester at Oklahoma A&M in Stillwater and made Corporal while in the ROTC there. The following summer he received a letter advising him that the National Guard had been called to Federal Service and he was to report to the Muskogee Armory for the Division's movement to Fort Sill for training.

Kilgore and his Division were at Fort Sill for about a year and then moved out to Camp Barklay, Texas. He was there on December 7, 1941, when Japan attacked Pearl Harbor and the U.S. entered World War II. He went on to Fort Benning, Georgia and graduated as 2nd Lieutenant in August 1942. His first assignment was as a platoon leader in Company G-302 of the 94th Division. He was later transferred to the 180th Infantry of the 45th Thunderbird Division. With the Thunderbirds, Kilgore shipped out to North Africa for amphibious training and then invaded Sicily in July 1943.

This Mediterranean island was strongly fortified by German troops including Hermann Goring's Panzer Division and a large contingent of Luftwaffe fighters and bombers. The Thunderbirds' first objective was to capture the airfield at Biscari, Sicily. They were expected to capture it in the first day, but it took three days of furious fighting to seize the airfield.

The 45th Thunderbirds continued across Sicily through July 1943 and captured the island in just over a month. Casualties were high for the Americans, but even higher for the enemy. Kilgore states, "We had met the best of the German and Italian forces, and had beaten them." General George S. Patton commended the Thunderbirds as being one of the best divisions in the history of American arms. The Sicilian campaign gave these brave soldiers their baptism of fire.

The 45th Division went on to fight in Italy and France and then in Germany itself. Charles Kilgore was a highly decorated member of this proud fighting force. Among his medals are the Silver Star, Bronze Star and Purple Heart. Kilgore's medals are proudly displayed at My Place BBQ on Gibson Street in Muskogee.

Local Seamstress Helped with War Effort

Ruth Dupree Johnson moved to Muskogee with her family in 1915 from the little town of Huttonville. Her father, Samuel Dupree, worked as a timekeeper for the Midland Valley Railroad. Her mother Lucille was a cook and housekeeper for a prosperous family and was active in the First Baptist Church and the local chapter of the National Association for Colored Women. The family lived in a "shotgun" style house on South 2nd Street near Coody Creek.

By age 11, Ruth had a job cleaning a shoe store on 2nd Street, which was the black business district of Muskogee at that time. But what Ruth really wanted to do was become a seamstress. She loved to study the Sears Roebuck catalog and then cut a pattern for herself or members of her family. She'd sew her designs on her mother's sturdy Singer sewing machine with its pump foot pedal.

After graduating from high school, Ruth attended one semester at Kansas State Teacher's College, but she did not continue because she couldn't give up her dream of being a seamstress. At age 18, she left Muskogee on a free rail pass from the Midland Valley Railroad and went to Chicago. Once there she made friends with some jazz vocalists who were heading to New York to work with Louis Armstrong. They took Ruth along with them.

Ruth took a job as a mechanic in the Brooklyn shipyard where battleships were being built for America's effort in World War II. A supervisor liked Ruth's precise work and noticed she had put "dressmaker" on her application. Knowing she'd be able to follow a blueprint pattern, he moved her to the position of cutting and fitting parts for the ship's smokestack.

She was soon in charge of the 5-man crew. They helped build the *U.S.S. Missouri*, the largest battleship built at that time. It was on the deck of the *Missouri* that the peace treaty with Japan was signed in 1945. The *Missouri* also saw action in the Korean Conflict and the Persian Gulf War. It is now a registered historical landmark and museum at Pearl Harbor, Hawaii.

After the war, Ruth was finally able to pursue her lifelong dream. At age 37, she entered the Traphagen School of Fashion in New York City. People had told her she couldn't get admitted because she was black, but she refused to let that stop her from trying. She was admitted to the prestigious school without any question or comment.

At the school, she worked for several celebrities and gained valuable experience in dealing with different personalities. Upon the advice of the school's owner, she moved to Los Angeles and set up a shop there. Soon she was designing and sewing for top Beverly Hills clients.

Ruth returned to Muskogee several years later to care for her elderly mother. She continued dressmaking from her home until her retirement. Ruth served as chairwoman of the Community Housing Resource Board in Muskogee and was awarded the Oklahoma Human Rights Award in 1986.

Indian Centennial Brought National Recognition

On October 14 and 15, 1948, the national spotlight shone on Muskogee as it hosted the Indian Centennial. This event was held to commemorate the one hundred years of progress of the Five Civilized Tribes in Oklahoma.

Prior to 1848, there were no "five civilized tribes." The tribes of the southeastern United States made treaties with the government as three tribes. The Choctaw and Chickasaw were closely related and always treated together. This was also true of the Muscogee (Creek) and Seminole tribes. But on October 12, 1848, the Chickasaw withdrew from the Choctaw Nation and established relations with the U.S. independent of that tribe. Later in the same month, the Muscogee Nation gave the Seminoles their own independent government. Thus the Five Civilized Tribes came into being in October 1848.

One hundred years later, in 1948, Muskogee celebrated this moment in history. The theme of the Indian Centennial was "One Hundred Years of Progress," and a number of events were scheduled over the two days of the centennial celebration. An Indian Arts Exposition was held at the Municipal Auditorium. Stage Coach holdups were re-enacted on Broadway between 2nd and 4th Streets. A parade ran from 12th and Okmulgee to Second Street, then back down Broadway to 17th Street. Floats and bands from schools, businesses, towns and tribes all over Oklahoma participated in the parade.

Bacone College played Connors State College in football at Athletic Park (where the Civic Center now stands) and Central High School played Okmulgee at Indian Bowl. Special Indian dances were also held at Athletic Park as well as a barbecue dinner. The U.S. Department of the Interior furnished elk meat for this meal.

On October 15, a special ceremony was held at the Post Office where an official Indian Centennial 3-cent stamp was released for sale. Congress had authorized the stamp to commemorate the centennial and it was to be sold first in Muskogee. It featured the seals of the Five Tribes with their names and the wording: The Five Civilized Tribes 1848-1948.

The seals of the Five Civilized Tribes along with the state seal of Oklahoma were also painted on the bricks of 3rd Street between Broadway and Okmulgee. According to different sources these seals had been laid out by historian Grant Foreman and Albert Hanson an engineer and artist. The seals were painted by volunteers. Though only a black and white photo exists of the seals, one account says the seals had a green background with a border of red, blue and black. The photo was taken from City Hall looking down on 3rd Street. The seals remained on the street until it was later resurfaced with asphalt.

The Indian Centennial was a major event in Muskogee's history, making the headlines of newspapers across the country. The events of the two-day celebration were broadcast on national radio and several magazines and film crews were also present. It was estimated that 10,000 people came to Muskogee for the parade and many dignitaries were part of the festivities. The Indian Centennial of 1948 served as a reminder that the city of Muskogee was and is the Indian Nations capitol of Oklahoma.

McClellan-Kerr Waterway Overcame Obstacles on the River

Navigation on the Arkansas River has always been recognized to have economic importance to Oklahoma.

Native Americans used the river to transport the furs they traded with the French and English. Those same European and American traders, as well as soldiers assigned to the frontier, utilized the river for moving furs and supplies.

As the region became more heavily populated, the river provided passage for travelers, including members of the Five Civilized Tribes who were forced to come to Indian Territory from their homelands in the southeastern United States.

Unfortunately, the Arkansas River was for most of this history a shallow waterway, choked with sandbars and debris. Its 400-plus miles between the Mississippi River and the Three Rivers region, descends gradually some 420 feet with occasional major drops in elevation such as the falls that give Webbers Falls its name.

All these factors made navigation on the Arkansas difficult. During dry seasons, it was often impassible. During wet seasons it could become a raging torrent. Business leaders had long searched for ways to make the river a more dependable, and economically profitable, natural resource.

Serious floods in 1923 and 1927 brought the need for work on the Arkansas River to the attention of Congress. The 1927 flood had washed out nearly every levee that had been constructed on the river and devastated towns in Oklahoma and Arkansas. The Arkansas River Flood Control Association was established and began to lobby Congress for funding to address the problem. Some funding was made available, but due to negative reports from the Corp of Engineers on the feasibility of river navigation, it took several more years before a waterway project could begin.

In 1946, lobbying by the Tri-State Committee (Arkansas, Kansas and Oklahoma) convinced Congress to pass the Rivers and Harbors Act authorizing the development of the McClellan-Kerr Arkansas River

Navigation System. Progress was halted by the Korean Conflict, and in 1954 it was put on a "deferred for further study" list. The build-up of sediment in the Arkansas appeared to make the project impossible.

Then Professor Hans A. Einstein, son of the well-known physicist, offered a solution. Deepen the river and it would flow faster. Faster water would prevent the build-up of sediment. The idea was tested on a stretch of river and found to work. The project was now feasible and by 1958 construction was being funding.

In 1968, the waterway was opened from the Mississippi River to Little Rock and barge traffic began along that stretch of the Arkansas. The full 440 miles to Catoosa were completed on December 30, 1970. And on January 3, 1971 the first barge arrived at the Port of Muskogee, carrying a load of steel.

Index

42nd "Rainbow" Division 95, 167
44th Infantry 33
45th "Thunderbird" Division 170, 171
88th "Cloverleaf" Infantry, 167, 168
180th Infantry 169
202nd Field Artillery 167
Act of Union 70
African, African American 27, 28, 63, 70, 87, 93, 94, 107, 113, 132, 157, 158
Afrika Corps 167
Agency Hill 12, 13, 94, 95, 163
Akins Cemetery 166
Alabama 10, 46, 55-58, 60, 65, 72
America, Americans 28, 29, 42, 43, 53, 60, 89, 99, 125, 148, 149, 152, 164, 166, 170, 172, 175
American Board of Missions 47
American Bridge Company 88, 89
American Profile magazine 150
American Revolution 43
American West 21, 27, 35, 49, 81
Anna, Santa 54
Apache 11
Appalachian Mountains 32
Arbuckle, Matthew 33, 37, 41, 110
Arkansas 35, 44, 46, 47, 74, 79, 80, 153, 175
Arkansas City, KS 31
Arkansas Post, AR 30, 33-35
Arkansas River 7-12, 15-18, 23, 25, 29-33, 35-37, 41, 46-48, 53, 55, 56, 58, 59, 61, 65, 66, 68, 69, 71, 72, 82, 83, 86, 88, 89, 92, 119, 137, 138, 141, 142, 146, 151, 168, 169, 174-176
Arkansas River Flood Control Association 175
Arkansas Territory 26, 34, 37, 42, 44, 58
Armstrong, Louis 172
Armstrong, William 71, 72

Army Rangers 40
Arrowhead Mall 90, 119
Astor, John Jacob 42
Athletic Park 126, 173
Atlantic & Pacific Railroad 66
Atoka County, OK 123, 124
Aunt Sally 31
Bacone College 26, 70, 114, 126, 173
Baltimore, MD 89
Bandit Queen 109
Baptist 112
Baptist Home Mission Society 94
Barbee, Ed 121, 122
Bartlesville, OK 123, 124
Baton Rouge, LA 153
Battle of Honey Springs 55, 79, 80
Battle of New Orleans 33, 34, 52
Battle of Pea Ridge 55, 79
Battle of Prairie Grove 79
Battle of San Jacinto 54
Bavaria 89
Baxter Springs, KS 81
Bean, Mark 26
Bean, Richard 26
Belle Point 35, 36
Bemo, John 68
Benedict, John 139, 140
Bennett, Leo 52, 129
Beth Ahaba Temple 90, 91
Better Homes & Garden magazine 152, 163, 164
Beverly Hills, CA 172
Big Bend, KS 29
Biscari, Sicily 170
Bixby, OK 141
Blackcoat 53
Blackstone, P.N. 100
Blue Mound 8
Blue Ridge Mountains 36
Blunt, James 79, 80

Board of Indian Commissioners 106
Bob 63
Bogey, Joseph 30, 41
Bonaparte, Napoleon 20
Bonnie & Clyde 165
Booker T. Washington High School (Tulsa) 158
Boone, Daniel 59
Boone, Nathan 58, 59, 64
Boudinot, F.J. 111, 112
Boynton, OK 134
Boy Scouts 148, 149, 157
Bradford, William 35, 36
Braggs, OK 50, 121, 166
Brainerd Mission 47, 73
Brearley, David 67
Bresser, Henry 149
Broken Arrow, OK 92
Booklyn Dodgers 126
Brooklyn, NY 172
Brown vs. Topeka Board of Education 114, 159
Buffalo Soldiers 49
Bushyhead, Dennis 49
Butler, Sam 121, 122
Butterfield Overland Mail Company 81
Byrne, Patrick 129
Caddo, Caddoan 8, 11, 17
Calf Creek Cave 7
Calf Creek People 7, 8
California 81
California Trail 81
Campbell, William 84
Camp Barklay 170
Camp Gruber 50, 95, 166, 167-169
Camp Kilmer 167
Canadian District 98, 100
Canadian River 10, 11, 17, 19, 56, 59, 61, 109, 110, 115
Cantonment Gibson 37, 49
Cashesegra 22
Catlin, George 64, 106

Catoosa, OK 32, 176
Central High School (Muskogee) 156, 169, 173
Chandler, OK 121
Chapman, Epaphras 37
Chattahoochee River 60
Chattanooga, TN 69
Checotah, OK 55, 92, 126, 137, 158
Checote, Samuel 105, 106
Cherokee Bill 104, 165
Cherokees, Cherokee Nation 23, 25, 26, 29, 36, 38, 43-45, 47-51, 52, 53, 58, 59, 68-73, 78, 79, 84, 85, 87, 88, 97-100, 113, 121, 129, 140, 150
Cherokee Female Seminary 74, 82, 140
Cherokee Male Seminary 82, 126
Cherokee Outlet 21, 62
Cherokee, The 71
Chicago, IL 88, 89, 148, 171
Chickasaw 157, 173
Choctaw 12, 29, 35, 43, 97, 173
Choska Bottoms 72, 119, 141
Chouteau, Auguste Pierre 19, 22, 28, 35, 41, 42, 52, 67, 124
Chouteau, OK 19, 121
Chouteau's Creek 88
Christie, Ned 104
Cibola 15
Cincinnati, OH 46
City of Muskogee 32
Civil War 8, 45, 48, 49, 55, 63, 66, 68, 69, 72, 73, 77, 79-81, 84, 86, 89, 95, 99, 103, 105, 106, 116, 130, 132, 139, 150
Claremont 22, 33
Claremore, OK 22, 121
Clark, William 32, 33
Cloud Creek 137
Cofield, John 134
Colbert's Ferry 81
Colorado 20, 81
Comanche 11, 17, 64, 65
Commercial National Bank 153, 159-161
Concharty Mountain 100

Confederacy, Confederate 26, 54, 70, 77-80, 105
Congregational Church 38
Congress 58, 94, 95, 120, 174, 175
Congressional Cemetery 70
Congressional Medal of Honor 167
Connors State College 162, 173
Convention Hall 145, 146
Coodey's Creek, Coody Creek 118, 171
Coodey, Ella 70
Coodey, Jane Ross 69
Coodey, William 69, 70
Cook, Bill 121
Cook Gang 121, 122
Cookson Hills 164-166
Cooper, Douglas 80
Coosa River 60
Coppinger, Rose 151, 152
Coppock, Benjamin 140
Coronado, Francisco de 15, 16
Corps of Discovery 32, 33, 42
Corps of Engineers 175
Council Hill, OK 57, 61
Council Oak 65, 66
Coweta, GA 54, 55
Creager, Charles E. 10
Creek Agency 31, 61, 67-71, 87, 90
Creek Agency, I.T. 67, 85
Creek Council 55, 56, 96
Creek Council House 57
Creek Lighthorsemen 105
Creek Oil & Gas Company 123
Creek Orphan School 115
Creeks (See Muscogee)
Creoles 28
Curtis Act 50, 113, 139
Dachau Concentration Camp 167
Dallas, TX 142
Dardenelle, AR 47
Davis, John 62

Davis, Sarah 87
Dawes Commission 58
Denison, TX 153
Denver, CO 145
Des Moines, IA 153
Detroit, MI 147
Dodge, Henry 64, 65
Doolin Gang 165
Dragoon Expedition 64, 65
Drake, Edwin 122
Drew's Ferry 83
Dupree, Lucille 171
Dupree, Samuel 171
Dwight Mission 45, 47, 48, 124
Dwight, Timothy 47
East Shawnee Cattle Trail 91
Ebenezer Mission 62, 63
Einstein, Hans 176
Elk Creek 80
Ellsworth, Henry 58
El Paso Stage Line 81
El Paso, TX 81
Emancipation Proclamation 132
England, English 18, 25, 60, 72, 175
Eufaula Creek High School 115
Eufaula Indian Journal 52, 115
Eufaula Lake 99
Eufaula, OK 10, 55, 97, 114, 115, 126, 154
Europe, European 11, 15, 16, 27, 30, 57, 167, 175
Evangel Mission 94, 113
Evans, Grant 120
Facility, The 31, 46, 47, 67
Fairfield Mission 124
Falls City, I.T. 23
Falls of the Verdigris 23, 30
Federal Reserve 161
Fern Mountain 13, 68, 72, 85-87
Fink, D.N. 153, 160
Finney, Alfred 47

First Baptist Church 171
First Creek Regiment 55
First Kansas Colored Volunteer Infantry 80
First National Bank of Muscogee 90, 129, 130
First U.S. Infantry 33
Fisk, Clinton 106
Fisk University 158
Five Civilized Tribes 11, 21, 26, 35, 52, 77-79, 82, 84, 93, 103, 113, 116, 123, 127, 129, 138, 173-175
Five Civilized Tribes Museum 94, 113
Flat Rock Creek 88
Flint River 60
Florida 10, 60, 65
Floyd, Charles "Pretty Boy" 164-166
Foley, C.E. 129, 135
Foreman, Carolyn 69
Foreman, Grant 13, 39-41, 45, 95, 161, 162, 174
Fort Benning, GA 170
Fort Blunt 79, 80
Fort Davis 70, 89, 90
Fort Gibson 22, 26, 28, 31, 33, 39, 42-44, 46-49, 52, 53, 58, 59, 61, 62, 64, 65, 70-72, 80, 81, 83, 85, 88, 111, 126, 161
Fort Gibson National Cemetery 45, 111
Fort Gibson, OK 48-50, 67, 112, 121, 169
Fort Gibson Post 111, 112
For Gibson Reservoir 119
Fort Leavenworth, KS 79
Fort Riley, KS 81
Fort Sam Houston, TX 167
Fort Scott, KS 79
Fort Sill 106, 170
Fort Smith 26, 31, 37, 44, 46, 81
Fort Smith, AR 10, 35, 43, 81, 103, 104, 115, 121, 122, 130, 142, 169
Fort Sumter 79
Foster, Charles 68
Fountain Baptist Church 63
Fowler, Jacob 27
Fowler, Paul 27

France, French 11, 16-20, 22, 25, 30, 175
Franklin, Buck 157, 158
Franklin, John Hope 157-159
Franklin, Mollie 158
French, Robert Mosby 35
From Slavery to Freedom 158
Frozen Rock, I.T. 69, 70
Fus Fixico 115
Galveston, TX 154
Garrett, W.H. 86, 87
Gary, Raymond 114
Georgia 10, 46-48, 54-58, 60, 62, 65, 165
Germany, Germans 167, 169, 170
Getty, J. Paul 124
Gibson Station, OK 88
Girl Scouts 156, 157
Glenn Pool 67
Glenn, Hugh 41
Gore, OK 26, 84
Gore, Thomas 84
Goring, Hermann 170
Graham, Richard 36
Grand Canyon 15
Grand River 8, 9, 21, 29-31, 36, 37, 41, 48, 59, 62, 82, 83, 110, 119, 123, 168
Grayson, George W. 85
Great Depression 50, 135, 161, 163, 165
Greeley, KS 79
Greene, William 107
Greenhill Cemetery 115
Greenleaf State Park 161
Green Peach War 105, 106
Gruber, Edmund 166
Guthrie, OK 56
Hall, Harry 66
Hall, James 66, 135
Hanson, Albert 174
Hardcastle, Stoney 109
Harjo, Chinnubie 114

Harrell Institute 137
Harris, C.J. 121
Harrison, Benjamin 120
Harsha & Spaulding Mercantile 126, 127, 138
Harsha, Laura, 125
Harsha, W.S. 137
Hartford, AR 140
Harvard University 158
Haskell Cemetery 121
Haskell, Charles 128, 142, 143
Haskell County, OK 8, 169
Haskell, OK 17, 72, 119, 120, 141
Hayes Mercantile 151, 152
Henry Kendall College 75, 113, 120, 126, 136
High Springs, I.T. 57, 61
Hinton Theater 115, 142, 143
Hinton, William 143
Hitchetee Town 73
Hitchita Trail 68
Hitchcock, Ethan Allen 139
Hitchcock, I.B. 99
Honor Heights Park 12, 95, 162-164
House of Kings 57, 119
House of Warriors 57, 73, 119
Houston, Sam 33, 48, 52-54, 69, 124
Houston, Temple 54
Houston, TX 54
Hoyt Bottom 110
Hubbard, Ernest 133, 134
Illinois 107, 139
Illinois Bayou 47, 48
Illinois River 19, 26
Illinois Station, I.T. 84
Indian Affairs Commission 58
Indian Arts Exposition 173
Indian Bowl 162, 173
Indian Centennial 173, 174
Indian Removals 10, 35
Indian Territory 10, 25, 35, 40, 42, 46, 48, 49, 51-53, 55-58, 60-

65, 67, 69,69, 72-74, 77, 79, 80, 84-87, 89-91, 93, 97, 99-101, 103, 104, 107, 112, 113, 116, 121, 123-133, 135-137, 139, 140, 143, 150, 154, 165
International Indian Fair 120
Irving, Washington 28, 40
Isparhecher 105, 106
Jack C. Montgomery VA Medical Center 13
Jackson, Andrew 33, 34, 36, 52, 61
James Brothers 165
Japan, 168, 170, 172
Jefferson Highway 84, 152-154
Jefferson Highway Association 153, 154
Jefferson, Thomas 20, 21, 24, 29, 152
Jenks, OK 141
Johnson, G.H. 142
Johnson, Ruth Dupree 171, 172
Jolly, John 48
Joplin, MO 153
July, Jim 110
Kansas 20, 23, 29, 31, 44, 77, 88, 98, 107, 116, 125, 142, 149, 175
Kansas and Arkansas Valley Railroad 49
Kansas City, MO 136, 142, 145, 149, 153
Kansas State Teacher's College 171
Katy Depot 94
Katy Pond 118, 119
Kearny, Stephen 64
Keetoowah 49
Kennard, Johnson 85
Kentucky 62
Kerr Lake 46
Kickapoo, OK 82
Kilgore, Charles 169-171
Kiowa, 11, 17, 65
Korean Conflict 172, 176
Koweta, I.T. 61, 113
La Cascade 19, 23, 24
La Harpe, Bernard de 17, 18, 27
La Louisiane 17-19

Latin America, Latinos 27
Leavenworth, Henry 64, 65
Leavenworth, KS 133
Ledbetter, James "Bud" 125, 133, 134
LeFlore County, OK 9
Lehigh, OK 123
Lewis & Clark Expedition 21, 29, 32, 33, 42, 52
Lewis, David 62, 63
Lincoln, Abraham 78, 86
Lindsay, OK 149
Little River 9
Little Rock, AR 46, 71, 176
Little Sister of Liberty 149, 150
Lochapoka Creeks 65
Long, Stephen 36
Los Angeles, CA 172
Lott, Nancy 68
Louisiana 11
Louisiana Purchase 20, 21, 29, 51, 152
Louisiana Territory 20, 34
Louisville, KY 32
Low, Juliette Gordon 156
Lovely County, A.T. 43, 44
Lovely's Purchase 23
Lovely, William 23, 36, 43
Lower Creeks 54-57, 60, 61
Loyal Party 105
Luck, H.C. 167
Mackey Salt Works 26
Madden Mercantile 121
Madden, Tom 122
Madison, Charles 146
Manard, OK 19
Manhattan Construction Company 166
Manitoba 153
Marquette, Jacques 19
Marsh, Hugh 143
Marshall, Thurgood 159
Martin, Judge 64

Martin, Matthew 64, 65
Masons, Masonic Lodge 73, 91
Mayes County, OK 8, 9, 62
Mayflower, The 86
Mazie, OK 25, 26, 37, 112, 138
McAlester, OK 154
McArthur, Douglas 167
McClellan-Kerr Navigation System 32, 174, 175
McCoy, Isaac 62
McGinnity, Joe 126
McIntosh, Albert 56
McIntosh, Chilly 55, 67
McIntosh, Chinubbie 56
McIntosh County, OK 73, 157
McIntosh, Daniel 55
McIntosh, Roley 55, 61, 63
McIntosh, Waldo 56
McIntosh, William 54-56, 60, 61
McCurtain County, OK 9
McWilliams, Sam 121, 122
Meagher, Thomas F. 68, 102, 103
Menard, Pierre 19
Meredith, E.T. 152
Methodist 106, 112, 137
Mexico, Mexican 11, 14-17, 27, 53, 54, 59, 104
Miami, OK 154
Middleton, D.H. 92
Midland Valley Railroad 140-142, 171
Minerva Home for Girls 113
Mississippian Mound Builders 8, 9, 21
Mississippi River 8, 9, 18-20, 22, 32, 34-37, 46, 56, 60, 67, 145, 153, 175, 176
Missouri 12, 22, 41, 79, 103
Missouri Compromise 20
Missouri-Kansas & Texas Railroad (Katy) 69, 87, 88, 90, 92, 93, 114, 136, 158
Missouri River 32
Mistletoe Troop 156
Monroe, James 20

Moore, Augusta Robertson 74, 96, 119-121
Moore, Napoleon B. 119-121
Morris, OK 165
Mule Shoe Ranch 119, 120
Murray, William 143
Muscogee (Creek), Creek Nation 8-10, 12, 28, 31, 46, 54-56, 58-63, 65-67, 72, 74, 75, 79, 85, 92-94, 96, 100, 105, 107, 113-115, 120, 121, 129, 132, 137, 173
Muscogee Station 82, 89
Muskogee and Seminole Live Stock Association 100
Muskogee Civic Center 126, 173
Muskogee Chamber of Commerce 138, 141, 160
Muskogee Commercial Club 138
Muskogee Cotton Oil Mill Company 117
Muskogee County, OK 8, 9, 17, 100, 138, 159, 165
Muskogee Garden Club 163, 164
Muskogee Historical Society 13
Muskogee OG&E Power Plant 69
Muskogee Oil Refinery 123
Muskogee, OK 10, 12, 52, 56, 67, 68, 81, 82, 85, 90, 91-96, 100, 102, 104, 107, 108, 113, 114, 116-121, 123, 124, 126, 127, 130, 131, 134, 136, 137, 139-143, 145, 146, 149, 153, 154, 156, 157, 159, 160, 163, 166, 169, 171-174
Muskogee Phoenix 52, 161
Muskogee Times-Democrat 12, 155
Muskogee Union Railroad 141
Muskoke 10
Muskoke Baptist Church 62
My Place BBQ 171
Nancy Taylor #1 124
Natchitoches, LA 81
National Association for Colored Women 171
National Banking Act 127, 129
National Register of Historic Places 124
Nation, Carrie 125
Native American 11, 19, 21, 22, 27, 36, 42, 43, 56, 59, 72, 97, 106, 112, 114-116, 122, 124, 138, 175
Ned 63
Needles, Thomas 129

Nellie Johnstone #1 124
Neosho, The 47
Neosho River 53
Neosho Salt Works 25, 26
New England 38, 86
New Jersey 167
New Mexico 15, 21
New Orleans, LA 17, 20, 28, 42, 46, 67, 71, 152, 153
New York City, NY 163, 172
New York Harbor 150
New York Yankees 126
Nicks, Eliza 45
Nicks, John 43-45, 49
Nicks, John Quinton 45
Nicks, Sarah, 44, 45
Nicksville, A.T. 44, 45, 48
Ninth U.S. Cavalry 49, 106
Nivens Ferry 83
North Africa 170
North America, Americans 8, 16, 32
North Carolina 43
Northeastern State University 140
North Fork 59
North Fork Town, I.T. 61
Nuttall, Thomas 24, 33
Nuyaka, I.T. 105, 113
Nuyaka Mission 120
Oak Cemetery 35
Officer's Circle 45
Ohio 75, 147, 166
Ohio River 37, 46
Okay Airplane Company 148
Okay, OK 23, 28, 53, 67, 147, 148
OK Auto Manufacturing Company 147
O-K Truck 147, 148
Oklahoma 6-8, 10, 15, 16, 18-21, 25, 27-30, 38, 40, 41, 43, 44, 49, 51, 52, 53, 62, 67, 81, 82, 84, 93, 95, 114, 117, 123-126, 128, 133, 140, 143, 145, 149, 150, 153, 162, 164, 165, 168, 173-175
Oklahoma A&M 170

Oklahoma Bank Guarantee Law 128
Oklahoma Baptist Convention 63
Oklahoma City, OK 146, 149
Oklahoma Constitutional Convention 56
Oklahoma Enabling Act 143
Oklahoma Free State Fair 157
Oklahoma Human Rights Award 172
Oklahoma National Guard 169, 170
Oklahoma School for the Blind 50, 59
Oklahoma Territory 21, 54, 128, 143
Okmulgee District 105
Okmulgee, OK 58, 61, 82, 85, 92, 121, 126, 136, 165, 173
Old Faucet Well 124
Orpheum Theater 143
Osage 11, 12, 21-23, 28, 29, 33, 34, 36-38, 41, 43, 44, 52, 65, 68, 113
Osage Agency 22, 52
Osage River 12, 22
Osage Trace 22, 25
Ouachita Mountains 19, 47
Overland Transit Company 81
Owen, Robert 52, 129
Ozark Mountains 19, 36, 40, 47, 165, 166
Palmer, George 163
Panzer Division 170
Parker, Isaac 103, 104, 121, 130-132
Park Hill, OK 73, 74, 82, 113
Patterson, Augustus 146
Patterson Cotton Gin 116
Patterson, James 68
Patterson Mercantile 102, 126, 127, 136, 137
Patton, George 170
Pawhuska 22
Pawhuska, OK 148
Pearl Harbor, HI 166, 170, 172
Pennsylvania 122
Pennywit, Philip 46, 47
Perryman, George 66, 92
Perryman, James 105

Perryman, Josiah 66
Perryman, Lewis 66
Persian Gulf War 172
Peterson, Elmer 164
Phillips, William 49, 80
Pikes Peak 91
Pike, Zebulon 21, 25, 29
Pin Party 105
Pine to Palm Road 153
Port of Catoosa 176
Port of Muskogee 32, 36, 59, 176
Porter, Pleasant 12, 105, 129, 143
Posey, Alexander 9, 114, 115
Poteau River 9, 19
Powhatan 32
Presbyterian Church 45, 67, 91, 112
Price, Sterling 79
Procter, George 143
Prospect Hill 93
Pryor Creek, OK 32, 34, 88, 141, 154
Pryor, Nathaniel 32-35, 41, 52
Quapaw 11, 12, 19
Quash 63
Quivira 15, 16
Rabbit 70
Rabbit's Ford 70
Railroad Day 140, 142
Rainbow Division Amphitheater 95
Rajer, Tony 150
Raven, The 53
Red Cross 120
Red River 11, 17, 18, 20, 64, 81
Reeves, Bass 132, 133
Rentiesville, OK 157-159
Rentie, William 157
Republic of Texas 20, 54
Rex Stoves 147
Rex, I.T. 147
Richards, Samuel 33, 34

Ridge, I.T. 141
Rifle Regiment 35, 36
Rio Grande 15, 17
Ritz Theater 143
Rivers & Harbors Act 175
Robb, A.W. 102, 129
Robertson, Alice 74, 75, 86, 94, 95, 107, 121, 140
Robertson, Ann Eliza 73-75, 86 119
Robertson, Grace 86, 96
Robertson Memorial Presbyterian Church 120
Robertson, Samuel 86
Robertson, William 74, 86, 119, 120
Rock Church 106, 137
Rockies, Rocky Mountains 20
Rogers, Diana 53
Rogers, John 43, 44
Rogers, Will 143
Rollin, David 63
Rome, Italy 167
Rommel, Erwin 167
Roosevelt, Franklin 167
Rosebud, SD 154
Ross, Daniel 49
Ross, John 69, 78
Ross, Joshua 120
Ross, Lewis 123
Ross, William 49
Rotary Convention 157
Route 66 154
Route 69, Highway 69   81, 138, 153
Rowland, Lura 50
Royal Arch Masons 73
Russellville, AR 45, 47
Ruth, Babe 126
Rutherford, Samuel 34, 35, 41
Sac and Fox Agency 82, 105
Sadler Arts Academy (Muskogee) 94
Salina, OK 19, 67
Sallisaw Creek 44, 47

Sallisaw, OK 19, 161
Sam Houston Park 50
Sanders, George 121, 122
Sand Springs, OK 7
San Francisco, CA 145
Santa Fe, NM 27, 81
Savannah, GA 156
Sawokla Cafeteria 94
Sawokla Farm 94, 95
Sawokla, I.T. 141
Schermerhorn, John 58
Sculleyville, I.T. 35
Searcy County, AR 7
Seattle, WA 145
Second Creek Cavalry 55
Secretary of the Interior 90, 139, 173
Secretary of War 36
Seminole 68, 70, 79, 100, 173
Senoia 54
Sequoyah 48, 161
Sequoyah Constitution 115, 143
Sequoyah County, OK 8, 9, 19, 44, 48, 165, 166
Sequoyah State Convention 56, 115, 143
Seton, Mrs. Ernest 157
Seventh Infantry 37, 43, 44, 110
Severs Block 128, 130
Severs, Frederick 92, 100, 118, 129, 135
Severs Hotel (Building) 92, 118, 126
Shackleford, James 104
Shawneetown, OK 82
Shoshone, Shoshonean 11
Sioux, Siouan 11
Sicily, Sicilian 170, 171
Six Bulls River 22
Sixkiller, Samuel 124
Smith Ferry 83
Smith, Paul 134
Smith, Thomas 36
Smithsonian Museum 13

Sondheimer, Alexander 90
Sondheimer, Eudora 90
Sondheimer, Joseph 89-91
Sondheimer, Samuel 90
South America 10
South Carolina 10, 60, 79
Spain, Spanish 11, 14-17, 19, 25
Spaulding, Homer 92, 135, 137
Spaulding Institute 137
Spaulding, Josephine Callahan 137
Spaulding Park 92, 120, 127, 137, 149, 153
Spiro Mounds 9
Spiro, OK 9
Spokogee, I.T. 10, 115
St. Johnsbury Academy 74
St. Louis, MO 27, 29, 33, 41, 42, 81, 89, 90, 136, 142, 145, 154
St. Paul, MN 153
Standiford, J.F. 107
Standing Rock 97-99
Standpipe Hill 94
Stanley Steamer Company 137
Starr, Belle 98, 104, 109, 110, 165
Starr, Sam 104, 110
Statue of Liberty 149
Stidham, George 68, 72, 73
Stidham, OK 68, 73
Stigler, OK 159
Stillwater, OK 170
Stokes, Montford 58
Stone Bluff, OK 141
Sulphur Springs, TX 137
Superintendent of Indian Affairs 35, 71
Supreme Court 114, 155, 159
Taft, OK 141
Tahlequah, OK 73, 78, 79, 126, 140, 149
Tahlonteeskee 47
Takatoka 48
Tallapoosa River 60
Tawakoni 11, 17, 18

Tennessee 34, 53, 69, 158
Tennessee Volunteers 34
Tenth U.S. Cavalry 49
Texarkana, AR 73
Texas 11, 17, 20, 53, 54, 64, 65, 81, 87, 91, 93, 98-100, 116, 132, 153, 170
Texas Convention 53
Texas Rangers 121
Texas Road 53, 65, 80, 88, 90, 93, 94, 111, 152, 153
Third Kansas Regiment 79
Three-Bar Ranch 100
Three Forks 23, 28, 30, 33, 35, 37, 42, 46, 47, 51, 52, 62, 71, 80, 119, 124, 140
Three Rivers 7, 8, 12, 16, 21-23, 25, 28-32, 34-37, 39, 41-43, 45, 51, 62, 67, 81-84, 88, 91, 95, 97, 100, 113, 116, 117, 123, 135, 139, 152, 157, 161, 162, 166, 168
Tour on the Prairie, A 28
Trail of Tears 61
Trans-Mississippi Congress 145, 146
Traphagen School of Fashion 172
Treaty of Indian Springs 55, 60
Trumbo, A.C. 145, 146
Tulasi, I.T. 65, 66, 113
Tullahassee Mission 74, 86, 96, 113, 120
Tullahassee, OK 113
Tullahassee Road 68
Tulsa County, OK 7
Tulsa, OK 66, 141, 142, 149, 158, 168
Tulsa University 120
Tulsey Town, I.T. 61, 66
Turner, Clarence 92, 129, 135, 136, 142
Turner, Fred 143
Turner Hardware Company 94
Turner Opera House 142
Turner, Tookah, 137
Twin Territories 128, 143
Twin Territories Magazine 98, 99
Underhill, Wilbur 165
Union 70, 77, 78, 80, 105, 150

Union Agency 13, 52, 85, 93, 94, 97, 118
Union Mission 26, 33, 37-39, 62, 112, 113, 124, 138
Upper Creeks 56, 57, 60, 61
United States 11, 27, 34, 58, 59, 67, 75, 93, 104, 122, 129, 146, 170, 173
U.S. Army 61
U.S. Attorney General 121, 129
U.S. Cavalry 21
U.S.S. Missouri 172
United Way 91
Van Buren, AR 47, 103, 132
Venus 110
Verdigris Kid 121, 122
Verdigris River 19, 22-25, 28-30, 32, 33, 35, 36, 41, 42, 53, 56, 58, 61, 67, 82, 88, 89, 168
Vermont 74
Verner, Enloe 154-156
Veterans Hospital 95
Vian, OK 19
Victory Bus Line 166
Vinita, OK 141
Virginia 32, 34, 46
Wagoner County, OK 8, 9, 88, 138
Wagoner, OK 90, 126, 162
Wainwright, OK 162
Waite, Stand 78
Wapanucka, I.T. 123
Warner, OK 162
War of 1812 33, 34, 43, 53
Washburn, Cephas 47, 48
Washington, D.C. 13, 42, 52, 53, 69, 70, 72, 78, 96, 120, 121, 154
Washington Union 70
Washington University 154
Washita River 64, 65
Watson, Edgar 110
Waverly, The 47
Wealaka, I.T. 115
Wealaka Road 68

Webbers Falls, OK 19, 31, 46, 67, 83, 150-152, 169, 175
Webber, Walter 24, 26, 150
Western (Baseball) Association 126
Western Cherokees 23, 47, 48
West Point Military Academy 41
West Virginia 107
Wetumpka, GA 54
Wewoka, OK 82
Whitaker, J.P. 149
White (Blanc) River 19
Whitefield, OK 109
Wichita 8, 11, 16, 17, 21, 22, 34, 65
Wichita, KS 142
Wichita Mountains 11, 65
Wigwam Neosho 53
Wilkinson, James 24, 29, 30
Willey, Charles 118
Williams, Paul 134
Winnipeg, Manitoba 153
Wisdom, Dew M. 52, 121
Women's Christian Temperance Union 125
Wooster University 75
Worcester, Ann 73, 74
Worcester, Samuel 73, 74
Works Progress Administration, WPA 161-163
World War I 95, 126, 147, 154, 156, 163, 167
World War II 51, 95, 157, 166-170, 172
Yale College 47
 YMCA 91
YWCA 91
Younger's Bend 109, 110
Zufall, Otto 118
Zuni 15

Glimpses of Our Past: Life Along the Rivers

Other Books by Jonita Mullins

Haskell: A Centennial Celebration

Glimpses of Our Past
A Look Back at Three Forks History

The Missions of Indian Territory
Journey to an Untamed Land
Look Unto the Fields

Contact Jonita Mullins
For book reviews and presentations,
women's conferences,
school lectures and historic tours

Okieheritage.com

Glimpses of Our Past: Life Along the Rivers

www.ingramcontent.com/pod-product-compliance
Lightning Source LLC
LaVergne TN
LVHW051555070426
835507LV00021B/2592